TOWARD PEACE
IN BOSNIA

INTERNATIONAL PEACE ACADEMY
OCCASIONAL PAPER SERIES

TOWARD PEACE IN BOSNIA

Implementing the Dayton Accords

Elizabeth M. Cousens
and Charles K. Cater

LYNNE
RIENNER
PUBLISHERS

BOULDER
LONDON

Published in the United States of America in 2001 by
Lynne Rienner Publishers, Inc.
1800 30th Street, Boulder, Colorado 80301
www.rienner.com

and in the United Kingdom by
Lynne Rienner Publishers, Inc.
3 Henrietta Street, Covent Garden, London WC2E 8LU

Library of Congress Cataloging-in-Publication Data
Toward peace in Bosnia : implementing the Dayton accords / Elizabeth M. Cousens
and Charles K. Cater.
    p. cm.—(International Peace Academy occasional paper series)
    Includes bibliographical references and index.
    ISBN 1-55587-942-X (pbk. : alk. paper)
    1. Dayton Peace Accords (1995)   2. Yugoslav War, 1991–1995—Peace.   3. Yugoslav
War, 1991–1995—Bosnia and Hercegovina.   4. Bosnia and Hercegovina—History—
1992–   5. Bosnia and Hercegovina—History, Military.   I. Cousens, Elizabeth M.
II. Cater, Charles K. III. Series.
DR1313.7.P43   T68   2001
949.703—dc21

                                           2001019008

British Cataloguing in Publication Data
A Cataloguing in Publication record for this book
is available from the British Library.

Printed and bound in the United States of America

The paper used in this publication meets the requirements
of the American National Standard for Permanence of
Paper for Printed Library Materials Z39.48-1984.

5   4   3   2   1

Contents

Illustrations

MAPS

TABLES

FIGURE

Foreword

David Malone

The civil wars of the 1990s tested the multilateral community's capacity to respond to mass violence and its aftermath to unprecedented degrees. Increasingly, practitioners and analysts have recognized the importance of developing strategies to consolidate and build peace beyond the mediation or conclusion of active armed conflict. Determining how the international community can best organize itself to engage in effective peacebuilding, however, remains an ongoing challenge.

This volume examines international efforts to implement the Dayton Accords that ended the Bosnian war in 1995 very much in this wider context. Elizabeth M. Cousens has closely followed political developments in southeastern Europe throughout the 1990s. She has also been involved since 1997 in an ambitious study of comparative peace implementation, conducted jointly by the Center for International Security and Cooperation at Stanford University and the International Peace Academy (IPA) and involving more than two dozen scholars and practitioners. By 2000, a thorough assessment of the international experience in postwar Bosnia seemed both feasible and useful. Consequently, I was delighted that Cousens tackled the challenge, drawing on both strands of her research, with the splendid result that you have before you. Her coauthor, Charles Cater, a colleague within IPA, drew on his own practical experience documenting persecution claims for Bosnian refugees with the International Rescue Committee (IRC), as well as on previous research on civil conflicts.

This particular research and policy development project made excellent use of IPA's niche as an independent institution close to the United Nations and several relevant regional organizations. Many of the implementers in Bosnia shared their perspectives with the authors. So have many of their critics.

The IPA Occasional Paper Series, as with all IPA work, aims to serve both practitioners and scholars in offering analysis and conclusions that do not shy from raising troubling questions. Cousens and Cater do not suggest that easy answers are available to international actors attempting to implement welcome but often imperfect peace plans. However, they do identify major pitfalls that could be avoided in the future while highlighting the areas decisionmakers should worry about the most, both in drafting peace agreements and then in attempting to implement them.

For this, I am deeply grateful to them both. I am also very grateful to the United States Institute of Peace for generously funding the research involved.

Acknowledgments

We wish, first, to pay sincere thanks to those practitioners and analysts who agreed to be interviewed by Elizabeth M. Cousens between 1996 and 1999. In particular, colleagues at the United Nations Mission in Bosnia and Herzegovina, the Office of the High Representative, the UN High Commissioner for Refugees, the World Bank, the Organization for Security and Cooperation in Europe, and the International Crisis Group took much time and great care, when they had little to spare of the former and far too much of the latter. This study would not have been possible without their contributions. Any of our insights properly belong to them, while any errors in fact or analysis are, of course, our own.

Over the course of our respective work on Bosnia, many at the International Peace Academy have offered invaluable help, especially Florence Musaffi. To Karin Wermester, we owe an enormous debt for her tireless efforts to coordinate what became at its last stage an intercontinental publication. We also benefited from a superb series of interns at the IPA, including Peter Singer, Alicia Allison, Bei Hu, and Diana Van Walsum, whose hard work greatly facilitated our research and writing. To David Malone and John Hirsch, we owe profound thanks for their encouragement and support.

We would further like to thank our publisher, Lynne Rienner, and the rest of her team for their hard work, patience with geographically scattered authors, and exceptional professionalism.

We are also grateful for the energy and intellectual inspiration of our colleagues in a joint research project on peace implementation conducted by the IPA and the Center for International Security and Cooperation at Stanford University, especially Donald Rothchild and Stephen John Stedman. In addition, several colleagues very helpfully commented in detail on earlier drafts of our manuscript, notably Marcus Cox and Mats Berdal.

A very particular and personal thanks is owed by Elizabeth to two individuals who helped shape an early interest in and commitment to matters Balkan: Susan Woodward, who from first meeting has been not only a mentor and a much admired colleague but also a dear friend; and Jan Øberg, whose unceasing commitment to conflict resolution and reconciliation remains an inspiration.

Likewise, Charles would like to thank Bob Carey and the staff of the International Rescue Committee.

We also gratefully acknowledge those institutions that financially and intellectually supported this project, beginning with the United States Institute of Peace, which made this publication possible, and including the Ford Foundation, the John D. and Catherine T. MacArthur Foundation, and the Carnegie Corporation of New York, all of which supported our related work on Bosnia and on peacebuilding more broadly.

Finally, though acknowledgments in an Occasional Paper offer a frail and inadequate way to do so, we wish to pay tribute to Mr. F. T. Liu. For years, he graced the IPA with his wit, insight, and wisdom. His knowledge of the United Nations, peacekeeping, and the intricacies of world politics was breathtaking, and we gained much from the far too little time spent in his presence. His was a remarkable spirit—he will be sorely missed.

—*E. M. Cousens*
—*C. K. Cater*

Introduction

By the end of 1999, the enormous international effort to implement the peace agreement that ended Bosnia's civil war in November 1995 had gone on longer than the war itself. Two basic concerns animated international activities in 1995: first, that war would not resume; and second, in the absence of war, that Bosnia would rebuild for itself a just peace, which international observers by and large considered a multiethnic one. Over five years later, neither concern has been conclusively resolved. Massive hostilities are unlikely to resume, but armed conflict over more targeted objectives remains a sufficient worry that international peacekeepers show no inclination to leave. More troubling, the parties to Bosnia's peace have resisted committing themselves credibly to a common political design for the country, leaving most of Bosnia's population under the governance of monoethnic authorities and the country's unity as yet unrealized.

Several years of peace implementation in Bosnia and Herzegovina have not been without significant accomplishments: several rounds of internationally certified elections have been held at national, subnational, and local levels; the power-sharing institutions designed to reunify the country are up and running, if with debatable effectiveness; nearly 650,000 of Bosnia's forcibly displaced citizens had returned by early 2000 to the country, if not primarily to their original homes;[1] significant portions of the country's infrastructure have been repaired; and not least, the military-on-military cease-fire that took hold at the end of 1995 has not been broken.

None of these achievements is without a subversive element, however. In this volume we argue, for example, that early elections militated against broader democratization and that military cease-fire in the absence of civilian security did as much to deepen certain of Bosnia's internal divisions as to heal them. Moreover, one cannot avoid tough questions about strategy and effectiveness when much of Dayton implementation remains to be realized, even after such massive and continuing expenditure of international personnel, resources, and energy.[2] Indeed, international implementers have faced iterated obstruction from Bosnian authorities, so much that even as they have drawn down their military presence, they have ramped up their civilian, political involvement. Several villages have even acquired special "envoys" because implementing local election results without sustained international pressure has proved so difficult.

To explain persistent divisions in Bosnian politics, one need not look far for explanations. To list just a few: a centuries-old history of interethnic antagonism and bloodshed; the "artificiality" of the Yugoslav state and the Bosnian Republic within it; an intensive recent war aimed at segregating populations; political leaderships whose commitment to an ongoing peace process in the country was questionable; and a peace agreement whose internal compromises—some would say contradictions—may have made it impossible to implement from the start. Most analysts would agree that each factor has played some role in Bosnia's postwar developments, even if they might disagree over their relative significance. In this sense, Bosnia's present state of affairs is what social scientists would call "overdetermined": too many explanations chasing a regrettably limited range of outcomes.

Within this matrix of contributing factors, however, we find that a disproportionate share of the explanation for Bosnia's current state belongs to strategic flaws in the international implementation effort. Between priorities set by involved governments and agencies and choices made by implementers on the ground, the process of implementation has needlessly helped consolidate the tripartite division of Bosnia. Indeed, the cumulative impact of these decisions has made it a much harder task to "implement Dayton" today than when the war ended.

In this volume we examine the first four years of international efforts to implement the Dayton Accords and argue the following: First, the Bosnian war ended with a deeply dissatisfying compromise among the warring parties to which they had only acceded under intense international pressure, especially from the United States. They could be predicted to try to turn the agreement to their respective aims during implementation or otherwise use implementation as an opportunity to revise or obstruct the settlement to which they had pledged themselves. An obvious implication was that international implementers would need a clear strategy for dealing with obstruction and an adequate set of tools with which to pursue such a strategy, very much including the capacity to exert sustained pressure or even coercion.

Second, the settlement reached at Dayton was sufficiently ambivalent between its separatist and integrationist components that it placed an enormous burden on implementers to decide their relative weight. This ambivalence was largely expressed in the tension among different provisions of the accord. Such tensions were not insuperable but could only be overcome by a serious, deliberate effort by a wide range of implementers to render their collective efforts coherent.

Third, international implementers actually enjoyed great *potential* influence in this regard. The agreement formally mandated to international third parties an extraordinary level of involvement and authority along multiple dimensions of postwar Bosnian politics. International parties also enjoyed leverage over the parties through their role as gatekeepers to membership in regional and international organizations and through their capacity to apply pressures and incentives of the type that got Bosnia's parties to agree to peace. Despite its constraints, the Dayton Agreement contained multiple opportunities for implementers to use these formal roles and informal relationships to overcome central weaknesses in the agreement itself, *provided that they recognized the need to do so and could rise above their own institutional limitations.*

Fourth, however, more opportunities were missed than seized by international implementers since late 1995. Early policy choices—such as the decision to decentralize implementation efforts among multiple international organizations, the unwillingness to use military resources in support of civilian implementation, and the sequencing of key provisions once implementation began—worked against Dayton's integrationist goals even while these were still publicly championed. The broader implementation effort was also weakened by competing strategies among key implementing actors and contributing governments, which were as often driven by bureaucratic and domestic considerations as authentic disputes about the best way to consolidate peace in Bosnia.

Finally, the principal result of such shortcomings was a growing gap between accomplishment and aspiration. This, in turn, generated great pressure on implementers to overcompensate in order to make up lost ground. The result has been an arrogation to international implementers of increasing authority to make binding decisions in Bosnian politics where the indigenous peace process fell short. Some have called this a "creeping protectorate," others an attempt to build "peace by fiat." By any name, the exercise of such powers by international parties in an essentially domestic context stands as an object lesson about the requirements of peace implementation under conditions as inhospitable as those of Bosnia.

*   *   *

This Occasional Paper proceeds along the following lines: Chapter 1 gives a short history of the Bosnian war and its settlement, emphasizing those factors that bear most heavily on the process of peace implementation. Chapter 2 focuses on the Dayton Agreement itself, its key terms as well as its ambiguities and the roles it devised for international implementing agencies. Chapters 3–8 treat what we argue are the six most critical aspects of implementation: security, refugees and internally displaced persons, economic reconstruction and development, reunification, democratization, and international authority. Chapter 9 sets criteria for evaluating Dayton implementation, reviews notable achievements and disappointments, and offers an explanation for this course of events. Finally, our conclusion, Chapter 10, reviews the policy lessons emerging from Bosnia, with a focus, first, on the likely effect on Bosnia's long-term peace process of such a heavy and protracted international presence and, second, on the implications of the Bosnian experience in the broader context of the rapidly evolving roles and missions of international organizations in the post–Cold War era.

NOTES

1. UNHCR Sarajevo, Returns Summary to Bosnia and Herzegovina from 01/01/96 to 30/04/00. Accessed 26 June 2000 online at www.unhcr.ba/Operations/Statistical%20package/1.htm.

2. In early 2000, the international military presence was scaled down to approximately 20,000 troops, and international police were maintained at just over 2,000, still considerable numbers in a country slightly smaller than West Virginia (51,233 km^2). Worryingly for prospects of long-term stability, one might draw a comparison to Sierra Leone in 2000, which was then attempting to stabilize a spectacularly fragile cease-fire: at one-and-one-half times the size of Bosnia, Sierra Leone was mandated by the UN Security Council a peacekeeping force of 13,000—one-quarter that of Bosnia's first implementation force, only two-thirds the size of its present peacekeeping strength, and presumably somewhat less well equipped than NATO-contributed troops. See http://www.un.org/Depts/dpko/unamsil/UnamsilF.htm, accessed 26 June 2000.

1

War and Settlement

Bosnia and Herzegovina found itself fully at war in the spring of 1992, after a year in which the Yugoslav federal state to which it belonged had come sequentially and violently apart. The Bosnian war was the third and most destructive stage of Yugoslavia's disintegration, following a short scuffle over Slovenia's secession and a serious, though also short, war over Croatia's departure. The dynamics of Yugoslavia's breakup bear heavily on Bosnia's evolving prospects for peace. Moreover, the circumstances that enabled the war to conclude and led to the signing of a peace agreement had concrete implications for what would be required to implement the agreement.

THE ONSET OF WAR

From at least the late 1980s, Yugoslavia's complex balance of powers among its six republics, two autonomous provinces, and six constituent nationalities had become increasingly untenable as well as fertile ground for competition among political leaders emerging in Yugoslavia's republics.[1] Long before it would have seemed plausible that Yugoslavia would literally dissolve, the political center of gravity had shifted significantly from the country's federal institutions to its republics and provinces (see map p. 20). Yugoslavia's third constitution, adopted in 1974, devolved authority along virtually every axis of institutional power: each republic now had its own central bank, communist party, educational system, judiciary, and, very importantly, police. The only institution that still operated exclusively at the federal level was the Yugoslav National Army (JNA), though it now acquired as commander-in-chief an eight-member, rotating federal presidency.[2]

In theory, the 1974 constitutional amendments were a progressive response to demands for local autonomy; in practice, they gave each republic an institutional toolkit to become a powerful rival to the central state and to one another. This unwieldy institutional framework was a godsend to any politician interested in building a personal power base, and Yugoslavia had several. The most ambitious of these appealed to national loyalties, grievance, and fears, particularly as the Yugoslav state's capacity to deliver basic goods shriveled and as Yugoslavia's economic and strategic status was called into question with the end of the Cold War.[3] Nationalism had long been the primary language of political opposition in Yugoslavia. National sentiment was also generally on the rise as the Cold War drew to a close, which Western governments and institutions greeted with a degree of, arguably, careless acceptance. By the end of the 1980s, as a result, conditions in Yugoslavia closely resembled those described by scholars as creating a high risk for ethnic conflict: declining overall and relative socioeconomic standards, weakening state institutions, social uncertainty and anxiety about "plausible futures," along with such longer-term attributes as a history of intergroup violence and affinities between groups on different sides of political or administrative boundaries.[4]

By 1990, when the first democratic elections were held in all six republics, nationalist politicians and parties were clear winners.[5] Serbian president Slobodan Milosevic had emerged as a champion of the Serb people, whose rights he encouraged them to believe were under assault everywhere from the province of Kosovo—which was 90 percent Albanian Muslim to 10 percent Serb—to the republic of Croatia, whose draft constitution in June appeared to grant rights only to Croats and not to the 12 percent of its population that was Serb. Slovenian leaders had openly declared their desire for national independence, directly challenging Milosevic in particular, who expressed a fierce commitment to keeping Yugoslavia together.[6] Croatia, meanwhile, was experiencing its own nationalist revival, electing the well-credentialed nationalist Franjo Tudjman as its first president of the post-communist era. Its new ruling party—the Croatian Democratic Union (HDZ)—replaced the emblems of Yugoslavia with Croatian symbols last seen during Croatia's collaboration with Nazi Germany. At the same time, hard-line Croatian Serbs had begun a militant autonomy movement whose core became the new Serbian Democratic Party (SDS). Bosnian politics had also turned in nationalist directions. The Muslim-dominated Party for Democratic Action (SDA) was founded in the spring, with Alija Izetbegovic as its president; and sister parties of the Croat HDZ and the Serb SDS were founded shortly thereafter.

Still more ominous, segments of the political population in Croatia and Bosnia had already begun to prepare for armed confrontation, both at the boundaries of the republics and within them. Within Croatia, the SDS, with support from Serbia proper, was building its own village-to-village military capacity in pursuit of what would soon be declared an independent "Republic of Serb Krajina."[7] By early fall of 1990, the Croatian government was secretly arming police and territorial defense forces and purging its security forces of Serbs in anticipation of JNA resistance to its secession. In Bosnia, Serb communities also began setting up village patrols that were increasingly militarized over the course of 1991 and 1992, when the JNA began discreetly transferring its Bosnian Serb troops back to Bosnia.

The immediate sequence of events that culminated in full-scale war in Bosnia was swift and brutal. Slovenia declared its independence on 25 June 1991, which it effectively won after an extremely short "war" with the JNA—more of a halfhearted police action conducted by military troops. Croatia simultaneously declared independence but met far more serious resistance from the JNA, Serb paramilitary units, and its own autonomy-seeking Serbs. As war in Croatia continued through late 1991, Bosnia's Serb and, to a lesser extent, Croat communities also began to mobilize for conflict. Serb leaders very vocally declared their intention to remain within the Yugoslav Federation or seek separation from Bosnia. Serb "autonomous areas" were set up in the fall, and a plebiscite was held in Serb areas to demonstrate Serbian opposition to Bosnia's secession from Yugoslavia. By early January 1992, Serbian president Slobodan Milosevic also began transferring Bosnian Serbs in the JNA back to Bosnia in anticipation of hostilities. Meanwhile, Bosnia's president, Alija Izetbegovic, and the SDA grew increasingly committed to Bosnian independence. When the European Community (EC) recognized both Slovenian and Croatian independence in January 1992, largely as a gambit to end the war in Croatia, it worked. Within two months, however, war had engulfed neighboring Bosnia.

Once Slovenia and Croatia had successfully seceded, Bosnia was left with a Hobson's choice: remain in a much smaller Yugoslavia that would be overwhelmingly dominated by Serbia and by implication its own large Serb minority, or leave the Yugoslav Federation, leaving Bosnian Serbs, and Bosnian Croats to a much lesser extent, analogously worried about domination by the country's Muslim plurality. Anxiety about the status of non-Muslim nationalities was not without basis, but it was also extravagantly stoked and manipulated by Serbian and Croatian leaders. Bosnia resembled the Yugoslav Federation uniquely among Yugoslav republics in its mix of nationalities, lack of an absolute

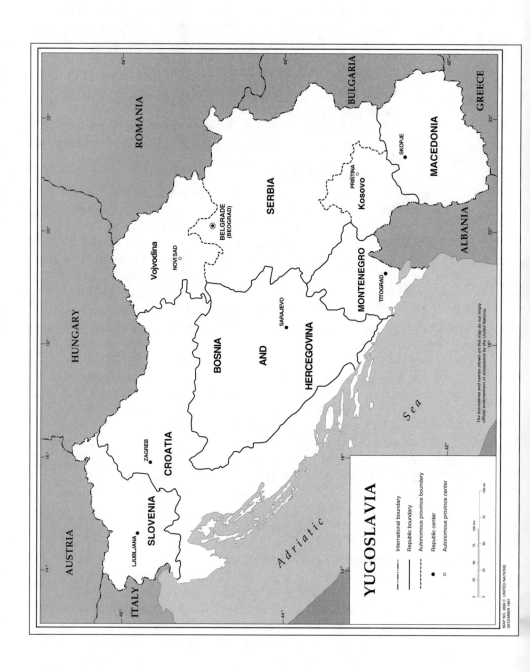

YUGOSLAVIA

International boundary
Republic boundary
Autonomous province boundary
● Republic center
○ Autonomous province center

0   25   50   75   100 km
0   25   50   75   100 mi

MAP NO. 3660 C UNITED NATIONS
DECEMBER 1991

The boundaries and names shown on this map do not imply
official endorsement or acceptance by the United Nations.

AUSTRIA
ITALY
HUNGARY
ROMANIA
BULGARIA
GREECE
ALBANIA

SLOVENIA
LJUBLJANA

CROATIA
ZAGREB

Vojvodina
NOVI SAD

BELGRADE
(BEOGRAD)

SERBIA

BOSNIA
AND
HERCEGOVINA
SARAJEVO

Kosovo
PRIŠTINA

MONTENEGRO
TITOGRAD

MACEDONIA
SKOPJE

Adriatic
Sea

ethnic majority, and intricate power-sharing formulas for managing ethnicity. Whereas the Slovenian population was close to 90 percent Slovene and Croatia 78 percent Croat, the Bosnian population was 44 percent Muslim, 31 percent Serb, 17 percent Croat, and 8 percent Yugoslav and other.[8] Within the framework of Yugoslavia, Bosnia had worked out a delicate balance of political power among these constituent nationalities. Once the Bosnian republic became an independent state, however, these constitutionally guaranteed relationships would be called into question: Croat, Serb, and Muslim status as constituent nations of the Federal Republic of Yugoslavia (along with Slovene, Montenegrin, and Macedonian) would not automatically guarantee them equal status as constituent nations of Bosnia. Uncertainty about national status in an independent Bosnia was only intensified by Izetbegovic's announcement of SDA opposition to national power sharing in favor of one-person-one-vote—a change that appeared to favor the larger Muslim population.[9]

In the event, Bosnia was recognized as an independent state by the European Community on 6 April 1992, one month after barricades were first raised in Sarajevo city streets, two days after President Izetbegovic ordered a general mobilization of Bosnia's territorial defense forces, and one day after Serb paramilitary forces besieged Sarajevo's police academy and the JNA seized its airport. In short, recognition occurred just as the country was being plunged into war.

During the next three and a half years, Bosnian government forces fought to preserve an independent, unitary state that would enjoy the same borders as the former Bosnian republic and ostensibly offer the same rights to its Serb and Croat citizens that they had enjoyed when Bosnia was a constituent republic of Yugoslavia. The government found itself at war on at least two fronts. From the beginning, it principally battled radical Bosnian Serbs, closely tied to and actively supplied by Serbia, who fought to "cleanse" large portions of Bosnian territory of non-Serbs and declare an independent Serbian republic (Republika Srpska) that might eventually join Serbia proper. Second, it faced Bosnian Croats, actively supplied by their own patron Croatia, who launched their own ethnically driven land grab in central and southern Bosnia in April 1993.

INTERNATIONAL PEACEMAKING EFFORTS

From 1991, the international community became intimately involved in efforts to settle the cascading conflict in former Yugoslavia, though at times the international community seemed as internally divided as the Bosnians. The European Community saw the Yugoslav crisis as a test case of its capacity for a common foreign and security policy—which proved possible, though only at a very low denominator of commonality. The United States, meanwhile, bemoaned European ineffectiveness but was unwilling to step into the breach. Initial debate revolved around whether the crisis in Slovenia and Croatia should be dealt with separately from the rest of Yugoslavia. The German government argued strenuously that recognition of the two republics' independence would solve the problem. Others, from European Community mediator Lord Peter Carrington through U.S. policymakers, countered that this approach would simply shift conflict to the remaining Yugoslav republics, with Bosnia first in line.[10] The German position prevailed, and Germany's widely perceived strong-arming of its European partners into recognition of Croatia and Slovenia set the tone for what would continue to be a contentious and destructively compartmentalized approach to Yugoslavia.[11]

International organizations and agencies also split over the question of impartiality toward the parties, especially in the Bosnian war. This division had complex elements. It began with competing analyses of the war's origins: Was the war caused by Serbian aggression against a newly independent Bosnia or by fratricidal cleavages within Bosnia? What was the nature of the belligerents: were all sides comparable in their violation of the laws of war or were there qualitative differences in culpability? Were rival forces composed of regular armies subject to identifiable chains of command or irregulars and thugs? International actors also split over the proper role of peacekeeping: Did UN forces facilitate peacemaking, or did they interfere with the need to back diplomacy with coercion? What were the implications of peacekeepers maintaining a conventional form of "neutrality" in the face of crimes against humanity or grave breaches of the laws of war? International actors were also divided between the diplomatic goal of a negotiated settlement and the human rights objective of a just one. This last was more than just a philosophical dispute; it was also a crudely operational one, with peacekeepers and diplomats on one side and human rights actors on the other.[12] Even within governments and institutions, mediators were capable of working at cross-purposes.[13] Partly as a result of such divisions within the international community, none of the series of peace plans developed by different international mediators prior to the Dayton talks was sufficiently backed by major international actors or sufficiently acceptable to the parties to become the basis for a comprehensive settlement.[14]

In the lead-up to Dayton, by contrast, international engagement in the conflict acquired an increasing coherence that, in turn, helped create and reinforce a changing balance of military power among the parties on the ground. These factors together made an agreement possible where it had earlier been elusive. A first element of this emerging coherence was the changing role of the United States, which began to recognize that it actually did "have a dog in this fight"[15] and developed for the first time in mid-1995 a serious strategy to bring about an end to the war. The United States built on a tactical alliance it had earlier brokered between Bosniacs[16] and Bosnian Croats in March 1994, when a Bosniac-Croat split was provisionally resolved by committing the two communities to a de facto military alliance to roll back Serb territorial gains and to a postwar "federation" in which they would be jointly governed.[17] Washington then added to its Croatian card a Serbian angle, recognizing Milosevic as the key broker on the Serbian side of the equation. The United States worked from the assumption that Bosnia would contain both the Bosniac-Croat Federation and a quasi-independent Republika Srpska (RS) and that both entities would be allowed to establish "special" relationships with neighboring Croatia and Serbia, respectively.

A second, arguably more critical element was a lurch into operational coherence among the various components of international Bosnia policy. Since the war began, international mediation, military, and humanitarian efforts had worked at cross-purposes. By mid-1995, they began to function more productively to support a common strategy to end the war. In large part, this coherence was forced upon the international community by the Bosnian Serb army. Previous calls for more muscular diplomacy in the Balkans had been persistently undermined by the vulnerability to reprisals of UN peacekeepers and other international personnel on the ground—primarily those deployed in six UN-designated Safe Areas.[18] That a way out of this bind had to be found became shamefully evident when Serb forces took hundreds of UN peacekeepers hostage following North Atlantic Treaty Organization (NATO) air strikes in May 1995.[19] It began to look increasingly likely that the United States would have to intervene in Bosnia simply for the unexalted task of safely withdrawing the troops of its allies. In the brutal event, this dilemma between the vulnerability of UN peacekeepers and the need for forceful diplomacy was eased when the enclaves of Srebrenica and Zepa fell to the Bosnian Serbs in July, removing along with the thousands of civilians expelled or killed, two of the least tenable deployments of UN peacekeepers in the country.[20]

Involved governments were now ready to align their respective military, humanitarian, and political efforts behind a common objective. In partial preparation for the possibility that the remaining UN peacekeepers would have to be withdrawn, the UN Security Council authorized a military Rapid Reaction Force in mid-June, which deployed around Sarajevo by the end of July. Foreign ministers of UN troop-contributing countries also ended the onerous "dual key" arrangement that required civilian UN approval of NATO action and agreed to use air power to deter an assault on Gorazde, the next Safe Area likely to be attacked.[21] In turn, the Clinton administration indicated that U.S. troops might be involved in enforcing whatever peace settlement was reached. Taken together, these decisions signaled a new unity in international diplomacy and a willingness to back it by force to an unprecedented degree.

A third element smoothing the path to Dayton was the international community's new willingness to use force, especially air power, as a partner to diplomacy.[22] By the end of summer 1995, obstacles to the use of NATO air power had been removed with the repositioning of UN Protection Force (UNPROFOR) troops, which were forced to depart from Srebrenica and Zepa and voluntarily left Gorazde.[23] Bosnian Serb forces also provided NATO with a rationale for air strikes by unleashing a mortar attack on 28 August that killed thirty-seven people in Sarajevo's marketplace.

Finally, the most powerful pressure to reach settlement arguably came from the dramatically changing military balance on the ground between the spring and fall of 1995, itself in no small way a product of U.S. efforts, which brought the territorial holdings of the warring parties into remarkably close alignment with the proposed basis for negotiation.[24] Starting in May, Serb forces suffered a series of defeats at the hands of the Croatian and Bosnian armies that significantly changed their calculus at the bargaining table and that also resulted from a new level of U.S. commitment to the Croatian military, which was being openly trained by nonofficial U.S. advisers. On 1 May, the Croatian army retook Serb-occupied territory in Western Slavonia, defying resident UN forces in that "UN Protected Area."[25] On 4 August, the Croatian army launched Operation Storm, an offensive that toppled the self-proclaimed "Krajina Serb Republic" in just two days, sending close to 150,000 Serb civilians fleeing into Serb-held Bosnia and Serbia.[26] Through the early fall, the Bosnian army in turn advanced dramatically on Serb positions. European Union (EU) negotiator David Owen described the situation from September this way: "Thereafter, day by day, the map altered."[27]

Alongside NATO's air campaign, the Bosniac and Croat military gains rapidly established the conditions necessary for a settlement, including the status of remaining Serb holdings in Croatia. By early September, talks in Geneva led to an agreement that the basis for settlement was a political subdivision of Bosnia into two coequal "entities" and a territorial split with 51 percent under Bosniac-Croat control and 49 percent under Bosnian Serb control.[28] By 20 November, three weeks of proximity talks at Wright-Patterson Air Force Base in Dayton, Ohio, produced a comprehensive agreement among all three warring parties and their regional guarantors. Not all parties to the conflict actually signed the agreement: by prior arrangement, Serbian president Milosevic signed on behalf of the Bosnian Serbs; Croatian president Tudjman's endorsement was analogously seen as a commitment to deliver hard-line Bosnian Croats who might not have felt sufficiently represented by the Bosniac-Croat Federation.[29] The resulting General Framework Agreement for Peace in Bosnia and Herzegovina (GFAP) was formally signed in Paris on 14 December.

When the war ended, more than half of Bosnia's 4.3 million citizens had been displaced, either as refugees in host countries (1.2 million) or as internally displaced persons within Bosnia's external border (1 million); roughly 250,000 were estimated dead or missing; and more than 200,000 were wounded, including 50,000 children.[30] Communicable diseases had increased between two- and fivefold, and infant mortality had doubled.[31] Physical and economic losses were severe, with total replacement costs of the country's destroyed assets estimated by the World Bank to be between $15 billion and $20 billion.[32] Industrial production, which made up the bulk of Bosnia's prewar economy, was reduced to between 5 and 10 percent of prewar levels;[33] up to 80 percent of agricultural equipment was destroyed; and between 2 and 4 million landmines littered the country, including large portions of productive farm and forest areas.[34] Bosnia's capacity for energy generation had been reduced by more than half and coal production by more than 90 percent; transportation, telecommunication, educational, and health infrastructures were heavily damaged; and more than half of the country's housing stock was either destroyed or unusable. At the end of the war, unemployment reached 90 percent, and per capita gross domestic product (GDP) dropped nearly three-quarters to $500 in 1995.[35]

SETTING THE STAGE FOR IMPLEMENTATION

Several features of the war and its conclusion would bear heavily on the prospects for peace implementation. First, the conflict in Bosnia was interdependent with the process of state formation in other former

Yugoslav republics, especially Croatia; its resolution would remain so, indicating an unavoidably regional dimension to peace implementation. Second, the rapid escalation of conflict in Bosnia was due partly to uncertainty about the boundaries of the political community within which basic rights would be guaranteed and the preemptive mobilization of ethnic groups that ensued; to the extent that such questions remained unresolved by the peace agreement, one could expect similar violence to continue. Third, the war occurred at the earliest stages of Yugoslavia's democratization, after a first round of multiparty elections but before most other ligaments of a democratic polity could be established or strengthened. The nature of the warring parties was also somewhat, if not fully, authoritarian, which remained the case in 2000. Fourth, in prosecuting their respective war efforts, the movement of civilian populations was an important instrument, as was the use of police and extramilitary groups, and both would come to have their peacetime equivalents. Fifth, coercion played a critical role in ending the war. This coercion was both external, in the form of NATO air strikes and high-stakes diplomatic pressure from outside governments, and internal, in the form of the Bosniac-Croat ground offensive. Sixth, such coercive instruments could only be effectively applied after greater operational coherence had been achieved among international actors in the field. Finally, the intervention of international parties was decisive, both in helping to produce a new balance of forces on the ground and in pressuring parties to sign an agreement about which they were ambivalent at best.

As a result, the Bosnian war did not end with a "mutually hurting stalemate" but with what is better called a "coerced compromise." What seems most decisive in bringing the parties to an agreement was the rapidly shifting military equation on the ground, itself deliberately generated by international actors, along with ferocious pressure from interested governments, especially the United States. Until the 1995 Croat and Bosniac advances, Serb forces had held a commanding position territorially, having seized nearly two-thirds of Bosnian territory within the first month of the war—which made it exceedingly difficult to extract concessions on the basis of anything less—and controlling almost one-third of Croatia, in Western Slavonia, Krajina, and Eastern Slavonia. Rapidly, however, they lost all their Croatian holdings except Eastern Slavonia and appeared vulnerable even to the loss of Banja Luka and western Republika Srpska. Croat and Bosniac willingness to settle was more complicated. In their view, though this remains controversial, their forces were on the verge of military victory over Serb-held western Bosnia, which was only forestalled after intense pressure from U.S. mediators whose formula for peacemaking required a Serbian guarantee and, therefore, precluded a Serbian rout.

The central implication for peace implementation is clear: having been brought to the table by varying forms and degrees of coercion, the parties had little more than a tactical commitment to settle, making any resulting accord dependent on more than the will of the parties for its implementation. Any chance for implementation would depend on international third parties developing a peacetime variant of the political and military formula that they had used to produce the Dayton Agreement in the first place. To end the war, international third parties deployed the considerable forms of leverage they had always held in potential; to implement the peace, they would need to do the same, at least until conditions could be created that would exert an analogous effect on the parties and render the peace self-sustaining.

NOTES

1. The Yugoslav state comprised six republics (Croatia, Serbia, Bosnia and Herzegovina, Slovenia, Montenegro, and Macedonia); two semiautonomous provinces linked to Serbia (Kosovo and Vojvodina); and six constituent nationalities (Croatian, Serbian, Slovenian, Montenegrin, Macedonian, and Muslim, the last having become an official Yugoslav nationality with constitutional amendments in 1974).

2. Unique among the republics, Bosnia also had a collective presidency comprising two Muslims, two Serbs, two Croats, and one Yugoslav.

3. Among scholars of Yugoslavia, Susan L. Woodward most systematically treats the country's dissolution as an example of state failure, with particular emphasis on its inability to manage fiscal and economic challenges. See her *Balkan Tragedy: Chaos and Dissolution After the Cold War* (Washington, DC: Brookings Institution, 1995).

4. See Stuart Kaufman, "The Irresistible Force and the Imperceptible Object: The Yugoslav Breakup and Western Policy," *Security Studies* 4, no. 2 (winter 1994–1995): 281–329; David A. Lake and Donald Rothchild, *Ethnic Fears and Global Engagement: The International Spread and Management of Ethnic Conflict,* Policy Paper 20 (San Diego: University of California Institute on Global Conflict and Cooperation, January 1996); and Barry R. Posen, "The Security Dilemma and Ethnic Conflict," in Michael E. Brown, ed., *Ethnic Conflict and International Security* (Princeton: Princeton University Press, 1993). Each of these authors emphasizes situations of uncertainty and what Posen labels "emerging anarchy" (103) as critically enabling ethnic conflict. The concept of "plausible futures" is from Lake and Rothchild (8–9).

5. That these elections were not held Yugoslavia-wide but rather sequentially, republic-by-republic, itself contributed to the country's disintegration. Notably, Slovenia was the first to vote and Serbia the last. See International

Commission on the Balkans, *Unfinished Peace: Report of the International Commission on the Balkans* (Washington, DC: Carnegie Endowment for International Peace), p. 27.

6. Slovenia had expressed its intention to secede in 1989, and of all the moves toward independence, its made the most sense. It was the westernmost republic, nationally homogeneous, with its own language, and economically best poised to operate independently of the rest of Yugoslavia.

7. In August, Serb radicals declared independence, which they effectively retained until mid-1995 when the Croatian army, then better armed and trained, retook the region, expelling virtually all its Serb population.

8. Figures cited by Woodward, *Balkan Tragedy,* 33.

9. See Laura Silber and Allan Little, *Yugoslavia: Death of a Nation* (New York: TV Books, 1995), p. 209.

10. Silber and Little, *Yugoslavia,* 199–200.

11. Germany pushed this agenda over the objections of the UK and the Netherlands, in particular, by threatening to recognize the two republics unilaterally if the EC did not do so collectively. At a time when European unity seemed of paramount importance to Germany's fellow Europeans, this strategy worked. See Silber and Little, *Yugoslavia,* 197–201.

12. See Manfred Nowak's frank account of the contradiction between the diplomatic and peacekeeping components of international intervention in Bosnia and human rights efforts. As he reports, and as we argue in this volume, these two dimensions of international intervention in Bosnia continued to be at odds after Dayton. "Lessons for the International Human Rights Regime from the Yugoslav Experience," *Collected Courses of the Academy of European Law,* vol. 8, book 2 (The Hague: Kluwer Law International, 2000).

13. See Daniel Serwer's account of trying to broker a deal between Bosniac and Croat forces in the context of larger mediation efforts by Richard Holbrooke, "A Bosnian Federation Memoir," in Chester A. Crocker, Fen Osler Hampson, and Pamela Aall, eds., *Herding Cats: Multiparty Mediation in a Complex World* (Washington, DC: United States Institute of Peace Press, 1999), pp. 547–586.

14. Beginning with the "Carrington Plan" of 1991, which was designed to prevent the war from ever breaking out, these included the "Cuteiliero Plan" in March 1992 (both under the auspices of the European Community Conference on the Former Yugoslavia, or ECCY); the Vance-Owen Peace Plan of April 1993, which proposed a division of Bosnia into ten ethnically balanced cantons; the Union of Three Republics Plan; the Invincible Plan (all three generated by the EC/EU-UN International Conference on the Former Yugoslavia, or ICFY); and the five-nation Contact Group's proposals of July 1994, which were revived in the form of the Dayton Agreement. For accounts of the negotiating history, see Richard Holbrooke, *To End a War* (New York: Random House, 1998); David Owen, *Balkan Odyssey* (New York: Harcourt Brace, 1995); and Bertrand de Rossanet, *Peacemaking and Peacekeeping in Yugoslavia,* Nijhoff Law Specials, vol. 17 (The Hague: Kluwer Law International, 1996).

15. After U.S. secretary of state James Baker traveled to Belgrade and Zagreb on 21 June 1991 in an eleventh-hour effort to defuse the crisis over Croatia and Slovenia, he explained that the absence of U.S. interests in

Yugoslavia with the phrase: "We don't have a dog in this fight." Silber and Little, *Yugoslavia*, 201.

16. The term *Bosniac* is used in this book to refer to those Bosnians who have identified their own nationality or ethnicity as Muslim.

17. Following the March 1994 "Washington Agreement," Croatia allowed arms and equipment to slip via Croatia to Bosnian forces, while the U.S. consultants discreetly worked with the Croatian army.

18. A United Nations Protection Force was established in February 1992 to facilitate the cease-fire in Croatia and as a complement to ongoing international mediation efforts. UNPROFOR's mandate was subsequently extended to Bosnia and came to include responsibility for six designated "Safe Areas." The first Safe Area declared was Srebrenica. See UN Security Council Resolution 819, Document S/Res/819 (1993), pars. 1–4. The Safe Area concept was extended to Sarajevo, Tuzla, Zepa, Gorazde, and Bihac with UN Security Council Resolution 824, Document S/Res/824 (1993), pars. 3–4.

19. United Nations, *Report of the Secretary-General Pursuant to Security Council Resolutions 982 and 987*, UN Document S/1995/444, 1995. See also Stephen Engelberg and Eric Schmitt, "Air Raids and UN Hostages Mark a Turn in Bosnia's War," *New York Times,* 16 July 1995, p. A1.

20. Srebrenica fell on 12 July, six days after the Serb assault began. Zepa fell on 25 July. The assault on Srebrenica stands as one of the most atrocious events of the war. Between 5,000 and 7,000 Muslim men are estimated to have been slaughtered during the week in July in which the town was taken by Serb forces. Beyond the obvious responsibility borne by Serb authorities for this bloodletting, many others have been accused of contributory culpability: the commander of local Bosnian forces who never arrived to help defend the town, the UN authorities who never managed to order close air support when it was desperately needed, and the U.S. authorities who are alleged to have known in advance but done nothing to prevent the assault on the town. On the UN role, see David Rohde, *Endgame: The Betrayal and Fall of Srebrenica, Europe's Worst Massacre Since World War II* (New York: Farrar, Straus and Giroux, 1997); and United Nations, *Report on the Fall of Srebrenica,* UN Document A54/549, 15 November 1999). On what U.S. authorities may have known, see Charles Lane and Thom Shanker, "Bosnia: What the CIA Didn't Tell Us," *New York Review of Books* 43, no. 8 (9 May 1996): 14.

21. At the same time, UN peacekeepers were discreetly pulled out of the enclave. Silber and Little, *Yugoslavia*, 360.

22. Many explanations have been offered for the relative nonuse of force before August 1995, from questions about the legality of force through arguments over the utility of air power to domestic and bureaucratic pressures to refrain from greater military engagement. Legal authorizations to use force certainly existed, not least the provision for individual and collective self-defense in the UN Charter, though this was arguably contravened by the existence of a UN arms embargo on the region beginning in September 1991. Security Council Resolution 713, UN Document S/Res/713, 25 September 1991, par. 6, called for the embargo. In 1993, the Security Council drafted a resolution that was never adopted, which called for lifting the embargo against the Bosnian government on the grounds that it violated Bosnia's inherent right of self-defense. See UN Document S/25997, 29 June 1993. U.S. congressional advo-

cates of lifting the arms embargo also based much of their case on Bosnia's right to defend itself.

The UN Security Council Resolutions establishing the six Safe Areas in Bosnia had authorized the use of all necessary measures to protect them (Security Council Resolution 836). The first Safe Area declared was Srebrenica, in Security Council Resolution 819 (16 April 1993). The Safe Area concept was extended to Sarajevo, Tuzla, Zepa, Gorazde, and Bihac with Security Council Resolution 824 (6 May 1993). Security Council Resolution 844 (18 June 1993) authorized the military reinforcement of UNPROFOR.

Later authorization for close air support of UN peacekeepers also enabled the robust use of force. Finally, even baseline rules of engagement permitted UN peacekeepers to resort to force in self-defense, though rarely has this been interpreted to go beyond physical defense of the peacekeeper to permit defense of the peacekeeper's mandate.

23. David Owen describes the situation at the end of August 1995: "For the first time since the autumn of 1992 UNPROFOR was no longer spread out across the whole of Bosnia-Herzegovina and vulnerable to Bosnian Serb retaliation and hostage-taking. UNPROFOR was out of Zepa, Srebrenica and Gorazde. Bihac was now safe. There were no significant UN forces in Serb controlled areas anywhere in Bosnia-Herzegovina. . . . It was inevitable, therefore, that the UN and NATO would take action against the Bosnian Serbs for the mortar bomb attack, which was a flagrant breach of the heavy weapons exclusion zone in Sarajevo." Owen, *Balkan Odyssey,* 331.

24. U.S. and European mediators were advocating as a basis for settlement that Bosniac and Croat forces would hold 51 percent of Bosnia's territory and Serb forces the remaining 49 percent. The 51:49 formula had been floated by Contact Group negotiators in July 1994 but was rejected at the time. Owen, *Balkan Odyssey,* 279–286.

25. The UN Protected Areas (UNPAs), all in Croatia, were part of UNPROFOR's original mandate and were distinct from the Safe Areas later established in Bosnia.

26. Another 50,000 soldiers fled as well. Søren Jessen-Petersen, UN High Commissioner for Refugees (UNHCR) Special Envoy, remarks at joint UNHCR-IPA Conference, "Healing the Wounds: Refugees, Reconstruction and Reconciliation" (Princeton, NJ: 30 June–1 July 1996). Some subsequent estimates have put the total for civilians and soldiers at a higher level of nearly 300,000. For example, see UNHCR, *A Regional Strategy for Sustainable Return of Those Displaced by Conflict in the Former Yugoslavia,* 17 June 1998; and International Crisis Group, *The Balkan Refugee Crisis: Regional and Long-term Perspectives,* 2 June 1999.

27. Owen, *Balkan Odyssey,* 335.

28. Statement of Agreed Basic Principles. For more information, see Holbrooke, *To End a War,* 133–141.

29. In the person of Federation president Kresimir Zubak.

30. Displacement figures come from UNHCR Sarajevo, Statistical Summary, November 1998. Casualty figures come from World Bank, *Bosnia and Herzegovina: Toward Economic Recovery* (Washington, DC: World Bank, 1996), p. 10; and World Bank, *Bosnia and Herzegovina: The Priority Reconstruction and Recovery Program: The Challenges Ahead,* Discussion Paper no. 2 (2 April 1996), p. 68.

31. World Bank, *Bosnia and Herzegovina: The Priority Reconstruction*, 68.

32. World Bank, *Bosnia and Herzegovina: Toward Economic Recovery*, 10.

33. European Commission and World Bank, *Priority Reconstruction Program: Achievements and 1998 Needs* (April 1998), p. 43.

34. World Bank, *Bosnia and Herzegovina: The Priority Reconstruction*, 81.

35. The 1990 level was $1,900 per capita. It is illustrative to compare Bosnia's 75 percent drop to eastern European economies that had undergone a peaceful transition after the Cold War: for example, Russia's GDP dropped by 50 percent; Albania and Macedonia's by 40 percent; Bulgaria, Romania, and Slovakia's by 30 percent (World Bank, *Bosnia and Herzegovina: Toward Economic Recovery*, 9–10).

2

The Dayton Framework

The Dayton Agreement essentially had two goals: to end the fighting and to rebuild a viable Bosnian state. To accomplish the first goal, the agreement detailed an elaborate calendar of commitments for separating and drawing down the armed forces of the Bosnian Serbs on the one side and the Bosniac-Croat alliance on the other. In a separate understanding, the United States also committed itself to beefing up Bosniac forces in order to create an internal balance of power that would ostensibly deter any future attacks by Bosnian Serbs.[1] To accomplish the second goal, the agreement included a wide range of provisions from a postwar constitution through elections to preservation of national monuments. Dayton also promised to restore all living members of the prewar population to their original homes, thus reestablishing the demographic base on which the postwar state could take root. Toward these twin grand objectives, the accords committed the international community to an ambitious and intricate set of roles throughout the process of implementation. These roles were also highly decentralized, which would make it that much harder to maintain any degree of policy coherence once implementation began.

KEY PROVISIONS

As a text, the Dayton Agreement consisted of a short "General Framework Agreement" in which the parties pledged to "welcome and endorse" the concrete provisions outlined in eleven substantive annexes.[2] The first of these covered "military aspects" of the settlement; the rest covered what are usually referred to as the "civilian" provisions, though this military-civilian dichotomy reflects less the inherently mili-

33

tary or civilian content of each particular provision than it does the authorized roles of third-party implementers.

Ending the Fighting

Dayton's military annexes principally secured the cease-fire line between Serb forces and the Bosniac-Croat alliance and thereby stabilized the territorial allocation of the country between them (49 percent Serb to 51 percent Bosniac-Croat alliance, Annex 1-A). Forces were to be separated along either side of an "Inter-Entity Boundary Line" (IEBL) dividing Republika Srpska from the Bosniac-Croat Federation (see map p. 35), and the parties accepted a detailed calendar of obligations governing cessation of hostilities. The parties agreed to a modest package of regional arms control and confidence-building measures (Annex 1-B) and pledged to cooperate completely with all international personnel, explicitly including those working with the International Criminal Tribunal for Yugoslavia (ICTY).[3] No provisions were made for the possibility of renewed hostilities between Bosniacs and Croats within the Federation.

The settlement was territorially vulnerable at two major points. First, the Bosniac-majority town of Gorazde that had been a Safe Area during the war was connected to the Federation by only a narrow spit of land. Second, the northern town of Brcko, to which both Serbs and Bosniacs laid primary claim, sat astride the even narrower Posavina land corridor that connected western and eastern Republika Srpska. Gorazde was treated within Annex 1-A largely as a matter of territorial demarcation that would be guaranteed by outside implementers. The situation at Brcko was more intricate. The town had been seized and held by Bosnian Serbs since the spring of 1992, when they drove out the bulk of the Bosniac and Croat population and sought—without success—to expand the 5-kilometer-wide land corridor between the two halves of the Serb republic. Before the war, Brcko's population was 87,332 and very mixed (44 percent Muslim, 25 percent Croat, and 21 percent Serb). Afterward, the population was displaced and divided, with around 30,000 in Brcko town proper and 99 percent Serb and about 63,000 in the immediately surrounding area who were 90 percent Bosniac.[4] The area was perceived as strategically critical for both sides: to take Brcko away from Serbs would effectively cut Republika Srpska in half; to give it to them would, beyond sanctioning ethnic cleansing, deprive the Federation of access to the Sava River and the trade and communications links that it represented. Because negotiations at Dayton were unable to settle the Brcko question, the dispute was

BOSNIA AND HERZEGOVINA

CROATIA

18°   19°

N. Gradiška

Danube   Vinkovci   Bač. Palanka

V. Kladuša
Šturlić   Bosanska   VOJVODINA
Varoška-   Dubica
Rijeka   Bosanska   Previc
45°   Bosanski   Gradiška   Derventa   Odzak   Šid   Srem   45°
Tržac   Novi   Prijedor   Prnjavor   Metrovica
Ivanjska   Brčko   Bogatic
Bihać   Bosanska   Piskavica   Banja Luka   Gradačac
Krupa   St. Rijeka   Vošavka   Doboj   Vučkovci   Bijeljina   Sabać
Sanski Most   Miljanovci   Gračanica   Srebrenik
Bos.   Sanica   **REPUBLIKA SRPSKA**   Teslić   Raduša   Ugljevik
Petrovac   Ključ   Krupa-na   Maglaj   Tuzla   Krstac   Loznica
Vrbasu   Maslovare   Zavidovići   Banja
Mrkonjić   Skender-   Mladikovine   Sprela   Kovljača
Grad   Vakuf   Žepče   Banovići   Zvornik
Titov Drvar   Sipovo   Jajce   Orahovačko   Zenica   Kladanj   Kamenica   Cerska   SERBIA
Gračac   Bos.   Polje   Vareš   Vlasenica   Konjević
Grahovo   Turbe   Travnik   Olovo   Bratunac
Pucarevo   **REPUBLIKA**   Srebrenić
Ervenik   Vitez   Breza   **SRPSKA**
Knin   Glamoč   Busovača   Sokolac   Žepa
44°   Kupres   Gornji   Fojnica   Kiseljak   Bajina Bašta   44°
Vakuf   Vogošća   Rogatica
CROATIA   **BOSNIAC-CROAT-FEDERATION**   Sarajevo
Drniš   Livno   Rumboci   Prozor   Tarčin   Pale
Šibenik   Prisoje   Duvno   Hrasnica   Višegrad
Sinj   Raško   Jablanica   Konjić   Goražde   Čajniče   Priboj
Divulje   Polje   Mesihovina
Trogir   Vinica   Foča   Pljevlja
Mali Drvenik   Čiovo   Split   Omiš   Imotski   G. Drežnica   Jasenjani   Kalinovik
Veliki Drvenik   Postire   Kočerin
Šolta   Brač   Makarska   Lištica   Mostar
Hvar   Vrgorac   Ljubuški   Blagaj   Nevesinje
Pakleni Otoci   Hvar   Medugorje   Gacko
Šćedro   Stolac   Avtovac
Svetac   Vis   Opuzen   Metković   43°
43°   Blato   **MONTENEGRO**
Biševo   Korčula   Peljašac   Bileća   Nikšić
Sušac   Lastovo   Peninsula   Trebinje
16°   Mljet   Šipan
Dubrovnik

ADRIATIC SEA

Herceg-   Podgorica
Novi   Kotor   Cetinje

The boundaries and names shown and the designations used
on this map do not imply official endorsement or acceptance
by the United Nations.   Budva   ALBANIA
Lake
Scutari

✪	National capital
○	Town, village
·–·–·	International boundary
··········	Inter-entity boundary line
–·–·–	Republic boundary
------	Provincial boundary
	Main road
	Secondary road
	Railroad
	Airport

**BOSNIA AND
HERZEGOVINA**

0 10 20 30 40 50 km
0   10   20   30 mi

17°   18°   19°   42°

42°

Map No. 3729 Rev. 2 UNITED NATIONS
January 2000

Department of Public Information
Cartographic Section

remanded to an international arbitrator for resolution within one year. Both sides, the Bosniacs with greater credibility, threatened to resume fighting should the Brcko decision not go their way.

On broader issues of public security and political violence against civilians, Dayton was comparatively weak. The settlement was manifestly more concerned with security between the entities than within them.[5] Nonetheless, the text did acknowledge security concerns beyond the narrowly military or the strictly interentity. It referred explicitly to extramilitary forces ("including armed civilian groups, national guards, army reserves, military police, and the Ministry of Internal Affairs Special Police") who had been in the vanguard of attacks on civilians both during the war and after, even as it implied that this concern was secondary to military-on-military conflict.[6] It further committed the parties to providing a "safe and secure environment for all persons in their respective jurisdictions" and to conducting law enforcement according to internationally recognized standards.[7] In addition, the accords authorized an International Police Task Force (IPTF) to monitor and help train Bosnia's police (Annex 11).[8]

Building the Peace

Dayton's "civilian" annexes covered everything else. National and entity elections (Annex 3) were to be held within nine months of the agreement's signing to launch Bosnia's new power-sharing institutions and give them democratic legitimacy.[9] The accords stipulated that the elections could only be held on schedule if "politically neutral" conditions pertained that ensured their freeness and fairness. A new constitution for the country (Annex 4) detailed the intricacies of national- and entity-level power-sharing arrangements, which were conceived as the formal mechanisms for managing tension between the pull toward unity and the push toward partition. The two entities retained significant autonomy under these arrangements, with exclusive authority over their own armed forces, internal affairs (including police), judiciary, and a wide range of social sectors. The entities also had exclusive right to taxes and duties collected on their own territory, which made the Bosnian state as a whole entirely dependent upon financial transfers from Republika Srpska and the Federation. Constitutionally separate from Dayton was the Bosniac-Croat Federation that had been established in 1994. Dayton included a short side agreement on Federation implementation but largely avoided confronting the possibility that the Federation might not cohere.[10]

To this politically and administratively complex environment,

Dayton promised that all 2.2 million of Bosnia's refugees and displaced persons could voluntarily return (Annex 7). Most of these people had, of course, been deliberately dispersed by one belligerent or another on the basis of their ethnicity. The accords thus obliged the parties to an extensive array of minority protection measures, from the repeal of discriminatory legislation and the suppression of hate speech to the agreement to refrain from intimidation and to prosecute any public authority who engaged in it.[11] Dayton also called for the parties to establish a commission to consider property claims and their just compensation.[12] Such provisions for the displaced had radical potential: given the ambitions of two of the warring parties and their chosen techniques for accomplishing these, full implementation of Annex 7 could amount to a flat-out reversal of the demographic course of the war.

Dayton further committed the parties to a full spectrum of provisions to protect human rights and called for them to establish a joint Human Rights Commission to ensure that these were adhered to (Annexes 4 and 6).[13] Worryingly, observers at Dayton reported that the parties agreed to their human rights commitments more easily than to any other provisions of the accords, perhaps reflecting the ease with which they anticipated being able to evade them.[14]

THE ROLE OF INTERNATIONAL IMPLEMENTERS

Military Responsibilities

The Dayton Accords outlined an extensive role for international actors in helping to implement the peace (see Table 2.1). Compliance with the accords' military provisions were to be supervised by a multinational Implementation Force (IFOR) led by NATO.[15] Authorized under Chapter VII of the UN Charter, IFOR was commanded by the North Atlantic Council (NAC), which was 60,000 strong at first deployment and was expected to complete its work by December 1996, or one year after Dayton's signing. Although its mandate encompassed all military provisions, IFOR's widely perceived primary role was that of a classic, if particularly well armed peacekeeping force: to separate armed forces, oversee the cantonment of troops and heavy weapons to agreed-upon areas, and stabilize the cease-fire.

Importantly, IFOR's secondary responsibilities ran the gamut of implementation activities. In overseeing compliance with the full range of commitments made under Annex 1-A, IFOR's responsibilities were linked to the parties' promise to ensure the safety of all civilians under

Table 2.1   The Dayton Agreement and Its Implementers

Annexes	Key International Implementers
1A Military Aspects	NATO-led IFOR
1B Regional Stabilization	OSCE
2 Inter-Entity Boundary Line (IEBL) and Related Issues	International Arbitrator
3 Elections	OSCE
4 Constitution	European Court for Human Rights, International Monetary Fund
5 Arbitration	
6 Human Rights	OSCE, Council of Europe, UNHCHR, European Court of Human Rights
7 Refugees and Displaced Persons	UNHCR
8 Commission to Preserve National Monuments	UNESCO
9 Bosnia-Herzegovina Public Corporations	EBRD
10 Civilian Implementation	International High Representative
11 International Police Task Force	UN

Note: See Appendix 1 for definitions of acronyms.

their respective jurisdictions, to provide humane and nondiscriminatory law enforcement, and to cooperate with the international criminal proceedings at The Hague. IFOR was also asked to support other components of international implementation, with specific reference to the return-related responsibilities of the UN High Commissioner for Refugees (UNHCR). Moreover, IFOR was expressly enjoined "to observe and prevent interference with the movement of civilian populations, refugees, and displaced persons, and to respond appropriately to deliberate violence to life and person."[16] This particular responsibility carried enormous significance if fully embraced. Consider it with reference to the text that immediately followed, in which NATO was authorized to augment its own role as the NAC saw fit and "without interference or permission of any Party, to do all that the Commander judges necessary and proper, including the use of military force to protect the IFOR *and to carry out the responsibilities listed above*."[17] IFOR's commander (COMIFOR) was also named the "final authority in theatre" regarding interpretations of all military aspects of the settlement.[18]

Related only minimally to IFOR's overtly military tasks were Dayton's provisions for arms control and confidence building, which were to be undertaken by the Organization for Security and Cooperation in Europe (OSCE), and for judgment over Brcko, which was to be decided by international arbitration (Annex 2, Art. V).

Civilian Responsibilities

In contrast to military responsibilities, the tasks of civilian implementation were parceled out annex by annex to lead agencies, though some tasks—like human rights—had no one formal steward, and some agencies—like the OSCE—had multiple responsibilities. The OSCE and the Provisional Election Commission (PEC) oversaw the preparation and conduct of elections. The UNHCR handled return of refugees and displaced persons. The UN peacekeeping operation that had been in Bosnia since 1992 was transformed into the backbone of an International Police Task Force to monitor and help reform Bosnia's police. Oversight of human rights provisions was collectively undertaken by the OSCE, the Council of Europe, the UN High Commission on Human Rights, and the European Court of Human Rights, and provisions for missing persons fell to the International Committee of the Red Cross (ICRC). The World Bank took the lead on postwar reconstruction, a role not articulated in the text of the agreement but widely acknowledged. Finally, the EU worked within the Federation to knit back together the divided city of Mostar, a responsibility that it had assumed before Dayton.[19]

International actors also became interim members of a wide array of Bosnian institutions and bodies, in many cases with decisionmaking authority (see Table 2.2). To spearhead its wide-ranging electoral responsibilities, the OSCE was asked under Dayton to establish a Provisional Electoral Commission to be chaired by its Head of Mission and with final authority over all of the body's decisions.[20] Three of nine seats on Bosnia's Constitutional Court were reserved for non-Bosnians, to be appointed to five-year terms by the European Court of Human Rights.[21] Bosnia's Central Bank was to be governed for its first six years by a non-Bosnian governor appointed by the International Monetary Fund. Within the country's new Human Rights Commission, the Ombudsman was a non-Bosnian for the first five years, appointed by the OSCE, and eight out of fourteen members of the Human Rights Chamber, including its president, were appointed for five-year, renewable terms by the Council of Europe. Three of nine members of the Commission for Real Property Claims of Displaced Persons and Refugees (CRPC), including the chair, were appointed for five-year renewable terms by the European Court of Human Rights; two of the five members of the Commission on Public Corporations were appointed by the European Bank for Reconstruction and Development; and two of five seats on the Commission on National Monuments were appointed by the UN Educational, Scientific, and Cultural Organization

Table 2.2 International Membership in Bosnian Offices

Office	International Appointees	Authority/Term	State Appointees	Federation Appointees	Republika Srpska Appointees
Provisional Election Commission (PEC) 7 members (later expanded to 16)	4, including the OSCE Head of Mission as chair	Chair's decisions are binding	1 (then 2, then 4)	1 (then 2, then 4)	1 (then 2, then 4)
Constitutional Court 9 justices	3, appointed by the European Court of Human Rights	5 years; thereafter, Parliamentary Assembly can amend selection process		4	2
Governor of the Central Bank	Appointed by the IMF	6 years			
Human Rights Ombudsman	Appointed by the OSCE Chairman-in-Office	5 years, nonrenewable; thereafter, Bosnian president			
Human Rights Chamber 14 members	8, appointed by the Council of Europe Committee of Ministers, including the president	5 years, renewable		4	2
Electoral Appeals Subcommission (EASC) 4 members	1		1	1	1
Joint Interim Commission	Chaired by the High Representative			4	3
Commission on Real Property Claims 9 members	3, appointed by the European Court of Human Rights, including the chair	5 years, renewable		4 (3- and 4-year terms)	2 (3- and 4-year terms)
Commission on Public Corporations 5 members	2, appointed by EBRD, including the chair	5 years, renewable		2	1
Commission on National Monuments 5 members	2, appointed by UNESCO, including chair	5 years, renewable		2	1
Independent Media Commission (IMC) 7 members	3 each, plus the IMC director-general			3	1

(UNESCO). In addition, a civilian High Representative was authorized to establish any new mechanisms or bodies he or she found necessary for civilian implementation.

Coordination

With so many international bodies responsible for implementing various components of the Dayton Accords, some means of coordinating their efforts was needed. The model adopted at Dayton was loose, particularly on the civilian side, indicating the desirability of coordination but not providing any actor with a serious mandate to achieve it (see Figure 2.1).

To coordinate the panoply of civilian efforts, Dayton authorized an international Office of the High Representative (OHR) to oversee civilian implementation.[22] The High Representative was to enjoy final interpretive "authority in theatre" of Dayton's civilian provisions, analogous to the COMIFOR's authority to interpret military provisions. Although the representative's role was textually coequal to that of COMIFOR, it was widely recognized that the High Representative would enjoy far less effective authority, particularly over other implementing agencies that reported separately to their respective governing bodies and had neither the habit nor the incentive to put their operational resources under the direction of someone else. With respect to fellow implementers, the High Representative had, at best, the leverage of the bully pulpit—to consult, inform, cajole, liaise, even hector, but not to direct, allocate, or spend, let alone hold accountable.[23]

More strategic oversight was meant to come from a newly established Peace Implementation Council (PIC) composed of implementation-friendly governments, to whom the High Representative would report.[24] The PIC was created out of the remnants of the International Conference on the Former Yugoslavia that had been in operation since August 1991 in order to generate sustained support for and give strategic direction to the implementation process. Comprising more than fifty governments, its principal body has been a Steering Board that aimed to strike a balance between including as many key governments as possible, especially major donors, and remaining small enough to be agile and decisive.[25] The five-nation Contact Group also provided an opportunity to harmonize the diplomatic efforts of its members and exert appropriate leverage on the parties, though its role declined relative to the PIC after 1996 largely because it did not include major donors.[26]

Figure 2.1 Relationships Among Major Implementing Agencies

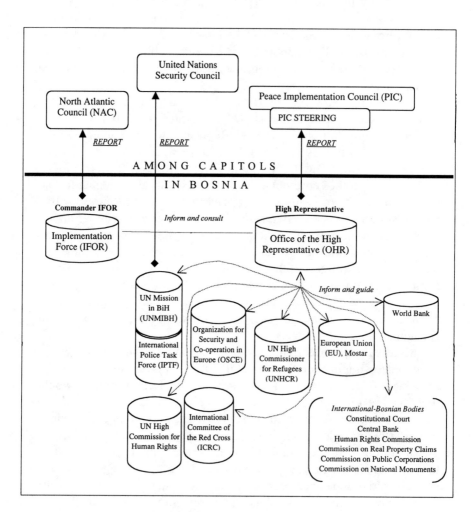

CONSTRAINTS UPON IMPLEMENTATION

From the beginning, those implementing Dayton had every reason to expect an uphill climb. Four major sets of challenges faced them.

The Parties

It was no secret that the parties to the Dayton settlement were ambivalent about signing and could be expected to try to obstruct implementation, at least tactically. Two of the belligerents—the Bosnian Serbs and the Bosnian Croats—did not even properly sign the agreement but rather were "represented" by the presidents of their respective patron states, Yugoslavia and Croatia. The Serbs got a demographically sweet deal (49 percent of Bosnian territory when they represented only 31 percent of the prewar population) but a territorially disappointing one. Their entity was effectively divided into two halves at Brcko; Sarajevo was highly unlikely to be open to them in any serious way; and as a result of the Bosniac-Croat offensive in late 1995, their population had been swollen by approximately 200,000 refugees. Serbia, meanwhile, offered Bosnian Serbs only diminishing hospitality along with a depressed economy and international isolation. Nonetheless, the agreement gave Serb authorities enough autonomy that they could effectively self-govern Republika Srpska territory. Whom they would end up governing was an open question, depending on the progress of refugee and internal return.

Bosnian Croats did comparatively well, sharing power and land within the Federation in significant disproportion to their population (17 percent of the prewar population), but their leadership was brazen in its lack of interest in real integration with the Bosniacs. Their hard-line constituency, centered in southwestern Bosnia, was publicly committed to the Croat "parastate" that they set up in the middle of the war (Herzeg-Bosna), which, they argued, deserved no less autonomy as an effective third "entity" than the Serbs. The Croat position was demographically complicated by the existence of Croat communities sprinkled throughout central Bosnia—often in towns that the war had left ethnically divided—but they also had a distinct advantage over the Serbs, sharing a long, porous border with Croatia, which backed them unambiguously and with far greater resources.

The Bosniacs were, in turn, deeply dissatisfied by the peace but desperate to see the war end. At Dayton, they were asked to cede almost half the country on behalf of a decentralized state whom many doubted would really survive. They also generally believed—as did Bosnian

Croats—that their forces had been on the verge of victory over the Serbs when the United States vigorously appealed to them to stop short of retaking western Republika Srpska. The Bosniac leadership accepted the Dayton deal with misgivings and, according to most accounts, only after promises were made to heavily invest in Bosnia's postwar reconstruction and to equip and fully train Bosnia's still-neophyte army. Although the Bosniacs maintained then, as they continue to do, that their preference remained a united and multiethnic Bosnia, the war had strengthened the position of hard-liners within the SDA, which led some to doubt the authenticity of their commitment to a unitary state. Indeed on all sides, the unsurprising effect of the war was to fortify nationalist voices and diminish moderate ones.

The Peace Agreement

That the peace agreement was deeply problematic was also no secret. Its calendar of obligations was dramatically unbalanced between a highly detailed military schedule and what can only be called a minimalist political one. Indeed, the only firm deadline on the civilian side was that national elections be held within nine months, a timetable that many argued at the time was unrealistic and even counterproductive. Other than deadlines, the settlement gave no direction to the parties or to implementers on the relative importance of its many and varied provisions, the need to set priorities among them, or the likely consequences should those priorities remain unestablished or unwisely set.[27] Instead of recognizing that such ambiguities might require a strategically integrated approach to implementation, Dayton proposed a model of third-party assistance that artificially segregated military from civilian—read "political"—components and that gave maximum autonomy to multiple international organizations to coordinate their own efforts voluntarily, a capacity for which they have never been particularly noted. The accords also depended upon a continuing level of international commitment that was not only unlikely to be sustained but whose evanescence was actually written into the text of the accords.

Perhaps most problematic, Dayton effectively offered no clear, single political outcome for the country. In this respect, it should more accurately be considered an "interim" than a final agreement, more akin to the Oslo Accords for the Middle East, where final status issues remained unresolved, than something like the Chapultepec settlement in El Salvador. Despite its 130 pages of detailed text, Dayton's mediators had crafted an accord based on a fundamental ambivalence between its partitionist and its integrative elements. On the one hand, Dayton stabilized lines of confrontation and derived political rights from them; on the other, it aspired to override such divisions, both from above—in its joint institutions—and from below—in its provisions for return. It also essentially neglected the question of *intra*-Federation conflict, which had presumably been resolved from 1994 on but which many anticipated as posing significant obstacles to peace implementation. That Dayton did not tackle all these issues did not make it fatally flawed, but it did mean that the settlement imposed on its implementers an enormous burden of interpretation and strategic coherence.

The Peacebuilders

A third set of challenges arose from the nature of the actors who engaged in third-party implementation: international organizations and agencies, donor governments and ministries, and nongovernmental organizations (NGOs). Each of these typically experiences operational kinks that will affect a peace implementation process, ranging from startup delays and coordination and information problems to resource scarcity. Such issues are not unique to Bosnia or even to peace implementation: they go with the territory of organizations, especially ones in which decisionmaking is collective and political as well as divorced from operations. That said, such traits are widely enough known that they can be explicitly factored into plans for implementation.

More problematic is the abiding tendency among such actors to compete for what might crudely be considered as implementation "market share." Rivalry over roles and turf has tended to characterize how organizations and governments approach their involvement in peacebuilding. Several factors encourage such competition: difference in organizational mandates, even to the point of contradiction; different methods of financing, forms of governance, and lines of accountability; distinct organizational cultures; and divergent conceptions of what constitutes legitimate forms of international engagement. As a result, questions about roles, responsibilities, and division of labor in achieving a common set of objectives—stabilizing peace, for example—are rarely answered simply by assessing comparative advantage among implementing agencies.

More commonly, lead roles are allocated and defined on the basis of institutional and national bargaining, which may sometimes be driven by merit but is often led by political factors. A few examples will suffice: the European Union was asked to "administer" the divided city of Mostar, more because European governments were willing to foot a large bill than because there was reason to think that they could advance the peace process between Bosniacs and Croats. The OSCE was asked to supervise Bosnia's elections instead of the UN, even though the former had no experience in doing so, largely because key member governments saw the UN as discredited by its peacekeeping performance during the war. For similar reasons, Dayton's crafters never seriously considered naming a UN Special Representative of the Secretary-General (SRSG) instead of a High Representative, despite the obvious logic of not starting such an office from scratch. Meanwhile, it was understood that the High Representative would always be European; one chief deputy was likely to be German and one American; and the OSCE Head of Mission would always be American.

Again, such patterns are not unique to peace implementation. However, in contrast to a purely peacetime development effort, for example, the stakes in peace implementation are risked in a much shorter time frame and are arguably higher. The remedy for such divergence among implementers is really twofold: policy coherence at the strategic level and operational coordination in the field, with capacity between them for real-time evaluation and course correction as needed. Given the Dayton Agreement's own cross-purposes at the strategic level, coordination among implementers in-country became even more important. Unfortunately for Bosnia and its implementers, mediators opted for a model of implementation that was divided (between military and civilian) and decentralized (among civilian provisions), with all coordination being essentially voluntary. Particularly given the recalcitrance of Bosnia's parties and the ambiguities in the political settlement, this choice was risky at best and negligent at worst.

The Political Commitment

A final issue centered on domestic political constraints within key governments—particularly the United States—and the open question of their stamina to see through a longer peace process than one year. Precisely because of its premature, ambiguous, and coerced quality, the Dayton settlement could be predicted to need a coherent, strenuous, *and sustained* form of engagement from major international actors. Getting such a commitment from the United States was of disproportionate importance, especially since European governments, burned by the experience of UNPROFOR, had refused to join any postwar implementation force without U.S. participation.

Many of those working on U.S. Bosnia policy recognized that peace in Bosnia would take time as well as troops.[28] Convincing the U.S. Congress to agree to any U.S. troop involvement, however, was

Table 2.3 The Dayton Agreement and Its Deadlines

Deadline	Civilian Obligations {annex/article}[a]	Military Obligations, Annexes 1A and 1B {annex/article}[b]
No deadline, *inter alia:*	• "The Parties shall provide a safe and secure environment for all persons in their respective jurisdictions." • "The Parties undertake to create in their territories the political, economic, and social conditions conducive to the voluntary return and harmonious reintegration of refugees and displaced persons, without preference for any particular group." {7/II}	• "Recreate normal conditions of life in Bosnia-Herzegovina" {1A/1}.
1–3 days		• Identify to authorities all "physical or military hazards" (mines, barbed wire, etc.) within Bosnia and Herzegovina {1A/V}. • Shut down air early warning and defense systems and fire control radar {VI}.
1 week		• Transfer and vacate selected positions along the cease-fire line in Sarajevo {1A/IV}. • Begin talks on confidence-building measures {1B/II}.
3 weeks		• List war-related prisoners to all parties and enable ICRC to interview prisoners at least two days before their release {1A/IX}.
30 days		• Disarm and disband armed civilian groups except authorized police {1A/II}. • Withdraw foreign forces {1A/III}. • Withdraw forces behind a Zone of Separation (ZOS) on either side of cease-fire line {1A/IV}. • Withdraw fully from cease-fire Zone of Separation in Sarajevo {1A/IV}. • Remove, dismantle, or destroy all mines, unexploded ordnance, explosive devices, demolitions, and barbed/razor wire from cease-fire ZOS and other areas from which forces are withdrawn {1A/IV}. • Do same in all cases required by the IFOR commander {1A/IV}. • Identify locations of all explosive devices in Bosnia and Herzegovina {1A/IV}. • Require parties to give Joint Military Commission specific information on status of their forces, including location, types, weaponry within 10 km of the cease-fire line, specifics on all surface-to-air missiles/launchers and anything else of a military nature required by the IFOR {1A/V}.

(continues)

Table 2.3 continued

Deadline	Civilian Obligations {annex/article}[a]	Military Obligations, Annexes 1A and 1B {annex/article}[b]
		• Release or transfer all prisoners {1A/IX}. • Begin talks on arms control and limitations on military manpower {1B/IV}. • Require parties to report their inventory of forces and arms {1B/IV}.
45 days		• In those areas where one entity is to transfer control to another, withdraw all departing forces and remove equipment, mines, obstacles, unexploded ordnance, demolitions, and weapons. Forces from the arriving entity may not enter the area for 90 days {1A/IV}. • Agree upon initial set of confidence-building measures {1B/II}.
3 months	• Amend all pre-Dayton constitutions in conformity with the new constitution of Bosnia-Herzegovina {4/IV}. • Establish a Commission for Displaced Persons and Refugees {7/VII}. • Establish a Human Rights Chamber {6/VII}.	• Require parties to refrain from importing any weapons during this period {1B/III}.
6 months	• Appoint arbitrators to settle the dispute over Brcko {II/V}.	• Withdraw all heavy weapons and forces to designated locations and demobilize all forces that cannot be held in those areas {1A/IV}. • Require parties to refrain from importing any heavy weapons {1B/III}. • Require parties to give a JMC specific and comprehensive information on the status of all their forces, including location, types, weaponry, and anything else of a military nature required by the IFOR {1B/V}. • Conclude arms control negotiations on numerical ceilings for forces and weapons {1B/IV}.
9 months	• Hold first postwar national elections {3/II} for 2-year terms. Hold local elections if desired (no specific deadline).	
1 year	• Determine Brcko dispensation as "final and binding" {2/V}.	
2 years, 9 months	• Hold second national election. This time, the results remain in effect for 4–5 years.	

Notes: a. Deadlines for civilian provisions were measured against the signing of the General Framework Agreement for Peace in Bosnia and Herzegovina on 14 December 1995.

b. Deadlines for most military provisions (and for Federation obligations) were measured against the official transfer of authority from the UN to NATO on 20 December 1995.

daunting, let alone in a mission that smacked of "nation building," "mission creep," or "quagmire." The twin shadows of Somalia and Vietnam were long, particularly in 1995 with a militarily untested president and a presidential election just one year away. To get congressional support, the Clinton administration had to ensure that the Dayton Agreement contained a quick exit for U.S. troops, thus the premise in the agreement and in public language surrounding it that the bulk of peace implementation would be accomplished by the end of 1996. As a result, many references were made to "keeping Dayton on track" and "sticking to the Dayton schedule" (see Table 2.3, pp. 47–48).

The question of stamina or lack thereof had two general dimensions: First, would the United States and other governments prolong their engagement in the event that it turned out to be necessary? Second—and this was a more subtle question—what signal did such public reticence send to the Bosnian parties and to the population? To the parties, whose manipulation of international mediators had been notably deft during the war, it suggested the merits of a waiting game. To the population, who had been disappointed by what they perceived as inadequate international efforts during the war, it suggested that the limits of the possible in postwar Bosnian politics would be set by Bosnian politicians and Bosnian politicians alone.

Whether Dayton was the best agreement that one could have made to end an ugly war is difficult to say. Dayton's mediators had cobbled together a flawed, possibly premature peace to stop a war whose humanitarian and political consequences had finally become unbearable to international observers. They accomplished what none yet had been able to—a cease-fire—amid daunting challenges. The critical question was whether implementation could compensate for such an unpromising beginning.

NOTES

1. This program was called "train and equip" and has been run from its inception by the same private company, Military Professional Resources Inc. (MPRI), that gave technical assistance to the Croatian army during the war.

2. For the full text of the accord, see *General Framework Agreement for Peace in Bosnia and Herzegovina*, 14 December 1995 (hereafter, GFAP). Available online at http://www.ohr.int/gfa/gfa-home.htm.

3. Annex 1-B and Annex 1-A, Art. II, pars. 1–4. Arms control measures set a ratio of forces among the parties and their regional guarantors based on their respective populations and ostensible defense needs. From a baseline determined by the military capacity of the Federal Republic of Yugoslavia (FRY), armaments were to be reduced as follows: to 75 percent of the baseline for FRY, 30 percent for Croatia, and 30 percent for Bosnia. Bosnia's 30 percent

would, in turn, be allocated between the entities in a ratio of 2:1 (Federation to RS); Annex 1-B, Art. IV.

4. This is a prewar estimate from an internal document, UN Civil Affairs, Brcko. Postwar estimates of the population in Brcko town come from Task Force Eagle, Memorandum for Record, "Brcko Assessment," 22 May 1996; in the wider Brcko municipality, from UNHCR, "Brcko Municipality," March 1996, p. 3.

5. The parties were primarily obliged not to "threaten or use force against the other Entity" or engage in "offensive operations," which was defined as "projecting forces or fire forward of a Party's own lines." Annex 1-A, Art. I, par. 2(a) and Art. II, par. 1.

6. Annex 1-A, Art. II, par. 1.

7. Annex 1-A, Art. II, par. 3.

8. That there was no ready text or convention to outline internationally recognized standards of law enforcement became a sticking point in the first stages of implementation, and the IPTF found itself having to draft the rules to which Bosnian police—and international police monitors themselves—would subsequently be held accountable. Author interview, Sarajevo, November 1996.

9. The agreement required that the first round of balloting cover at least executive and legislative offices at state and entity levels: the three-person presidency of Bosnia; president of Republika Srpska; and the respective legislatures of Bosnia, Republika Srpska, and the Federation. It held open the possibility also of electing legislatures of the ten Federation cantons and more than 100 municipalities (Annex 3, Art. II, par. 2).

10. See *Dayton Agreement on Implementing the Federation of Bosnia and Herzegovina* (10 November 1995) and *Bosnia and Herzegovina: Constitution of the Federation* (18 March 1994). The Federation was divided into ten cantons, which represented a level of government between municipalities (the lowest level of government) and entities and state (the highest). Of the cantons, three were predominantly Croat, five predominantly Bosniac, and two heavily mixed.

11. GFAP, Annex 7, Art. I, pars. 1–3.

12. GFAP, Annex 7, Art. VII. Now called the Commission on Real Property Claims, this body was originally termed the Commission on Displaced Persons.

13. The constitution incorporated sixteen international conventions that the government elevated to a status equal with domestic law, notably including the European Convention for the Protection of Human Rights.

14. Author interviews with senior mediators, United States, 1996, 1997.

15. When IFOR's mandate was first renewed beyond December 1996, its name was changed to the Stabilization Force (SFOR).

16. GFAP, Annex 1-A, Art. VI, par. 3(c–d).

17. GFAP, Annex 1-A, Art. VI, par. 4.

18. Ibid., Annex 1-A, Art. XII.

19. An EU Administrator was established in 1994 for the city of Mostar, which was heavily damaged by Croat-Bosniac fighting in 1993 and is only marginally less divided today between its Croatian western section and Bosniac eastern section than it was during the war.

20. Annex 3, Art. III.

21. Decisions depended on majority vote, and the six Bosnian members were split between four from the Federation and two from the Serb republic.

22. From January 1996 to April 1997, the High Representative was former Swedish prime minister and EU mediator in Bosnia Carl Bildt; from April 1997 through August 1999, the office was filled by Spanish diplomat Carlos Westendorp; and since August 1999, the office has been held by Austrian diplomat Wolfgang Petrisch.

23. The High Representative's authority even over his or her own office has been questionable. Most posts within OHR are seconded by member governments; particularly at high levels, these are allocated as much on the basis of political horse trading as of anything else.

24. The High Representative was also obliged to convey his or her assessments regularly to the UN Security Council. See GFAP, Annex 10; and the first OHR Report to the Security Council on 14 March 1996 (available online at http://www.ohr.int/reports/r960314a.htm).

25. The PIC Steering Board consists of the G-8 (which amounts to the Contact Group plus Japan and Canada), the OSCE Chairman-in-Office, and the EU presidency. "Conclusions" of the Peace Implementation Conference in London, UN Document S/1995/1029 (12 December 1995), par. 3.

26. Major donors—Japan, in particular—were persistently displeased about their exclusion from the Contact Group, which the PIC's membership and structure was set up to remedy. Author interview, Sarajevo, August 1998.

27. Other civilian provisions have deadlines but, in practice, have been much less consequential, largely because they are more technical or more easily obstructed. Examples include the obligation to bring existing constitutions into conformity with the Dayton Constitution. GFAP, Annex 4, Art. XII, par. 2.

28. Author interviews with officials in the U.S. Department of State and Department of Defense, 1996, 1997.

3

Security

The first and central task of Dayton implementation lay in the field of security. The war left Bosnia with two broad security challenges: first, to ensure that the parties would not reengage one another's armed forces; and second, to extend the cease-fire to civilians and ensure that they were no longer targets of organized violence. Together, both security considerations had in some fashion to embrace the full spectrum of potential belligerents, or what the Dayton Accords labeled "all personnel and organizations with military capability." This included reservists, national guards, military police, internal security forces, and armed civilian groups as well as the "foreign forces" that were meant to be withdrawn within thirty days after the peace accords were signed. To round out the security picture, the parties were obliged to conduct law enforcement "in accordance with internationally recognized standards and with respect for internationally recognized human rights and fundamental freedoms."[1]

PEACE BETWEEN THE PARTIES

At the end of the war, the immediate task was to consolidate the recently reached cease-fire; the longer-term goal was to ensure that the parties would have neither the capability nor the incentive to return to war. Dayton most comprehensively addressed the former, with an elaborate calendar of obligations on the parties to sequentially draw down their forces. Compliance would be assured by the 60,000-strong NATO-led IFOR.[2] Dayton addressed longer-term stability through committing the parties to reduce levels of arms and troops and to embark on a series of confidence-building measures under the supervision of the OSCE.

Importantly, Croatia and Yugoslavia were also bound by arms control and stabilization provisions.

Outside the Dayton framework, a curious coalition of the United States and several Islamic governments pledged themselves to a program of military assistance to the Bosniac-Croat Federation in order to render its capabilities comparable to that of Republika Srpska. The so-called train and equip policy was meant to create an internal balance of forces that would either deter renewed Serb attacks or enable an effective defense against them if deterrence failed. Such a balance could, in theory, also allow for the timely exit of international peacekeepers.

Cease-fire and Separation of Forces

The first plank of international strategy to keep peace was to separate the armies of the parties. Under IFOR's supervision, the cease-fire was consolidated almost to the letter of Dayton's provisions by the end of 1996. Federation and Serb military forces were separated, cantoned, and progressively demobilized. The IEBL was also quickly stabilized, with a 2-kilometer buffer zone on either side known as the Zone of Separation (ZOS), along which international troops deployed heavily—indeed, more heavily than along Bosnia's *external* borders. There were multiple points along the IEBL that had to be adjusted in the field—for example, because the official line bisected small villages that were otherwise not divided—but these issues were quickly resolved within the first several months of 1996.[3]

IFOR also quickly embarked upon its routine inspections of troop and weapons cantonment sites, which SFOR continues to conduct. Active duty troops were reduced largely according to schedule from a wartime high of more than 300,000 to 86,000 in 1997, in a ratio of 2 (Federation) to 1 (Republika Srpska).[4] A related international priority was to ensure the removal of "foreign forces" from Bosnian territory, among which international peacekeepers were most nervous about mujahideen from Islamic countries who had come to join the Bosniac cause. These were declared to have been expelled according to calendar by mid-1996.[5]

Arms Control

The second element of Dayton's strategy to keep military peace was to lower the overall level of armaments within the region. As stipulated by Dayton, the Bosnian parties and their neighbors reached an arms control agreement within six months that set numerical ceilings on heavy weapons.[6] Ratios were established between its signatories as follows: 5 (FRY) to 2 (Croatia) to 2 (Bosnia). Bosnia's "2" would be the sum of the arms of the two entities since the state itself had no capability of its own. Indeed, it took until March 1997 for the Bosnian state to acquire inspection rights with respect to the entities, since the Florence Agreement of June 1996 reserved such rights for parties actually in possession of arms.[7] Within Bosnia, the ratio was set at 2 (Federation) to 1 (RS). In a revealing discrepancy in the attached "Statement of Voluntary Limitations on Military Manpower," the Bosnian state was accorded a personnel ceiling of 60,000, or just about *half* the combined troop levels of the two entities (111,000). The Florence Agreement did not address how the Bosniacs (the Army of Bosnia and Herzegovina, or ABiH) and the Bosnian Croats (the Croatian Defense Force, or HVO) would calculate their respective contribution to the Federation's ceiling, which was a sticking point until June 1997, when the two established a mutually acceptable ratio of roughly 2 to 1 (see Table 3.1).[8]

Table 3.1   Arms and Troop Limits in the Florence Agreement

	FRY	Croatia	Bosnia and Herzegovina			IFOR
					Republika Srpska	
Ratio	5	2	2	Federation [2]	[1]	
Manpower	124,339	65,000	60,000	55,000	56,000	60,000
Artillery	3,750	1,500	1,500	1,000	500	
Tanks	1,025	410	410	273	137	
ACVs[a]	850	340	340	227	113	
Aircraft	155	62	62	41	21	
Helicopters	53	21	21	14	7	

Note: a. Armored combat vehicles.

Despite some early confusion and allegations of mutual cheating, arms and troop reductions were largely carried out according to the Florence commitments by the end of 1997.[9] The parties had also carried out 185 mutual inspections between August 1996 and October 1997, which some saw as the kernel of a sustainable regime for mutual military oversight.[10]

The Train and Equip Program

Within the overall limits established by the Florence Agreement, the United States proposed to "train and equip" Federation military forces to send "an unmistakable message of deterrence" against future Serb aggression.[11] The preeminent strategy was to create an internal balance of power. According to James Pardew, Jr., the State Department official overseeing the train and equip program that began officially in mid-1996, "Long-term peace in Bosnia requires the creation of a military balance, and a military balance is achieved by a combination of arms control and adequate training and equipment for the Bosnian Federation."[12] A second purpose was to use Western assistance and relationships to supplant the ties that had developed between Iran and the Bosniacs over the course of the war. A third goal of the train and equip program was to use it as a vehicle for integrating the ABiH and HVO. Indeed, the program would only start after the Bosniacs had demonstrably severed their relationship with Iran and the Federation had passed at least a nominal unified defense law.[13] In 1997, there was even talk of involving the Army of Republika Srpska (VRS) in the program, largely as a confidence-building measure.[14]

Train and equip, which was subsequently renamed a military stabilization program, was to be run by 185 personnel from Military Professional Resources Inc. (MPRI), the firm that had assisted the Croatian army during the war.[15] Arms and financing would come from the United States and a group of moderate Islamic countries. The program's military assistance has been valued at more than $400 million annually.[16]

Train and equip essentially represented a revived version of a policy that had been advocated during the war: to arm the Bosniacs so that they could defend themselves. It was strongly criticized from the outset, especially by European critics who saw it as contradicting Dayton's arms control provisions and the broader need to dissuade all parties from pursuing political objectives through military means.[17] Opposition to it was so fierce that it was excluded from the text of the agreement. The Pentagon also reportedly opposed the plan, which partly led to its being run by MPRI instead of being integrated within the implementation mandate of IFOR.[18] Overall, the status of train and equip neatly represented the dilemmas of peacemaking and peace implementation: according to observers, Izetbegovic and the Bosniac delegation would have refused to sign at Dayton had they not been promised such a package; at the same time, however, the program offered one of the more powerful disincentives to the parties to abide by Dayton's integrationist elements. During the particularly fragile early years of implementation, many critics worried further that train and equip would increase the probability of renewed conflict.[19]

This program has demonstrated more success at equipping

Federation forces than at training them, at least as an integrated army. After several years, although there is some joint training and troops now wear common insignia, both armies in Bosnia remain effectively separate in significant respects—budgets, personnel recruitment and promotion, administration, and command structure—meaning that Bosnia as a whole is host to three armies.[20] Beyond the amounts received via train and equip, military budgets within the Federation—including both levels and sources of foreign military assistance—are not appreciably more transparent than those in Republika Srpska. The ABiH and HVO only established official liaisons with one another in June 1998.[21] Intelligence functions are fully segregated, and despite some attempts at joint threat assessment in 1998, there remains no common security policy within the Federation, let alone between the two entities.[22]

Ironically, the postwar concern among critics of train and equip largely centered on the Bosniacs. Even if the program did not outfit the Federation beyond established ceilings, it represented a dramatic improvement in the capabilities of the persistently underarmed Bosniacs, which many feared might encourage them to return to war, especially given the frustration of their offensive in 1995. As one senior SFOR officer put it, "We've given an awful lot of men a lot of guns and taught them how to use them better."[23] In this context, the source of stability was the continued presence of NATO peacekeepers: "Sure, there's a balance of forces," he argued, "but the fourth force is SFOR." Concern that train and equip would give Bosniacs both the incentive and the means to reignite armed conflict has subsequently ebbed for multiple reasons, including the evident staying power of international forces; increased numbers of refugees returning, which both eases pressure and makes land grabs more demographically complicated; and the unlikelihood of sufficient unity within the SDA to launch a serious offensive.[24]

Extramilitary Considerations

A serious gap in implementation, especially early on, involved the treatment of those extramilitary forces enumerated under Annex 1-A as possessing military capability. From the beginning, IFOR was adamant that as a military force it would not perform anything resembling a police task, and since extramilitary forces tended to target civilians, their activities fell ambiguously in between "military" and "civilian." For reasons of force protection, IFOR was also reticent even about deploying so as to provide area security. In the first eighteen months after

Dayton, IFOR and subsequently SFOR thus opted not to inspect any forces other than regular military even though the agreement explicitly authorized them to do so. During this time, paramilitary groups and internal security forces enjoyed a peculiar freedom of movement alongside the presence of tens of thousands of heavily armed international peacekeepers. Smartly enough, they challenged neither the IEBL nor the safe operation of NATO-led forces, which enabled this ellipsis in the execution of SFOR's mandate to persist.

SFOR began to change tack in August 1997, however, when it announced that Interior Ministry "special police" units in Republika Srpska would now be subject to inspections. Special police had long been suspected of holding secret stores of heavy weapons; more salient to the shift in SFOR policy, they newly posed a threat to Western policy and even SFOR itself. In mid-1997, the United States and other major Western governments exploited a rift developing within the Serb leadership to back an ostensibly more moderate alternative to Radovan Karadzic, the founder of the Pale-based SDS. Until that time, international isolation of the Serb entity was near-total: Serbs received all the opprobrium for having started the war and virtually none of the humanitarian or economic assistance flowing into Bosnia after it. By 1997, it was becoming increasingly clear that Dayton implementation depended on a new approach toward Bosnian Serbs.[25] If Serb areas were not opened up politically or revitalized economically, there was precious little hope of getting traction on Bosnia's joint institutions or enabling non-Serbs to return to their homes. Once Biljana Plavsic broke with the SDS with open Western support, it created new security concerns: she had to be shored up against hard-liners, who enjoyed substantial support among Serb security forces, and international personnel had to be protected from possible retaliation by Serb militants.[26]

At the same time, SFOR also showed new interest in apprehending "persons indicted for war crimes"—referred to by the unhappy acronym PIFWCs. In July, British forces moved against two major figures indicted by the International Criminal Tribunal for Yugoslavia at The Hague, killing one and wounding another.[27] Their action represented the first use of force by NATO for this purpose. Until that point, all indictees had either surrendered to the tribunal voluntarily, had been arrested by national police forces, or were at large. Since 1997, SFOR has lent its support more assertively to the apprehension of PIFWCs, detaining twenty-one alleged war criminals.[28]

Over time, IFOR and SFOR also began to accept, if reluctantly, the secondary assignments of their mandate that authorized them to give all forms of support to civilian implementation. These included providing area security for the return of refugees, protecting the investigations of the ICTY by guarding exhumation sites, patrolling with the International Police Task Force, and seizing radio and television transmitters broadcasting inflammatory content, as SFOR was authorized to do in 1997 by the North Atlantic Council. The challenge of providing public security also led to the authorization in August 1998 of a Multinational Specialized Unit (MSU), a small corps of *armed* police meant to fill the vacuum between SFOR and IPTF. Under SFOR command, enjoying SFOR's wide freedom of action, and made up of 380 Italian carabinieri, seventy Argentine gendarmes, and twenty-three Romanian military police, the MSU was expressly fielded to deal with crowd control, riots, and protection for minority returnees.

PEACE FOR THE PUBLIC

If Bosnia's war had been complex, it nonetheless had had brutally simple attributes, including the forced migration of populations based on their ethnicity, or what became known as "ethnic cleansing." In their respective aspirations to control swaths of territory and any political authority subsequently established, Bosnian Serbs and Croats—to an extent, even Bosniacs—violently displaced or killed members of other ethnic groups in their way. What was often forgotten in post-Dayton Bosnia was that victims of ethnic cleansing included self-described "Yugoslavs" and "Others," as they were denominated in the Yugoslav census. In all cases, assault on civilian populations was both an aim and an instrument of war. Their attackers were sometimes regular military; more frequently, they were paramilitaries, militias, and other irregular forces; and sometimes they were also police who at the end of the war were estimated to have swollen beyond their peacetime number by threefold.[29] As a result, public security in post-Dayton Bosnia was a concern of rather a different caliber than simply whether internal order could be restored.

Beyond IFOR's extramilitary tasks, the Dayton Agreement dealt with public security by calling for the UN Security Council to authorize the IPTF as an unarmed, UN civilian police (CIVPOL) mission run by an international commissioner, who would jointly report to the UN Secretary-General and to the international High Representative in Bosnia.[30] The broad purpose of IPTF was to reform Bosnian law enforcement in line with Western standards of policing. They were to be demilitarized (or more accurately, de-"paramilitarized"), culled of suspected war criminals, trained in accordance with international standards, and essentially depoliticized.

IPTF was initially given no investigatory or enforcement powers vis-à-vis the parties and only minimal capacity vis-à-vis other implementers.[31] The IPTF, which would be unarmed and was expected to number somewhere near 2,000 personnel, was instructed to help the parties rise to "internationally recognized" standards of law enforcement through a combination of support and oversight, though as the first IPTF commissioner noted, such standards had nowhere been codified.[32] Indeed, CIVPOL missions, like peacekeeping operations, rely upon voluntary contributions from member states and often have problems with adherence to such standards among their own personnel.[33]

Downsizing, Democratization, and Multiethnicity

One of IPTF's primary responsibilities was to assist in the draw-down of Bosnian police to levels to be established post-Dayton, a particular challenge given the suspicion that many demobilized soldiers and militia had simply been transferred into police ranks. In this, IPTF and the parties have been reasonably successful, though there is some concern that there are nonuniformed personnel who are illicitly on police payrolls.[34] By 1998, the Federation had reduced its combined police force from 32,750 to 11,500, and by early 1999, the RS police had drawn down below an agreed threshold of 8,500.[35] By the same period, the vast majority of officers in both entities had also undergone international courses in "human dignity" training and in "transitional" training.[36]

Less successful have been efforts to integrate police forces ethnically or otherwise render them responsive to citizens beyond those of their own ethnic group. Just to get officers to wear "neutral" arm patches on their uniforms within the Federation required years of arduous effort, and as late as 1999, some forces still sported partisan insignia.[37] It has been much harder to get forces to recruit minority officers or field joint patrols, and nearly five years after Dayton, all three police forces, run by three separate interior ministries, operate in effective isolation from one another through every level of administration. The obstacles to integrating police are complicated, however, and not solely rooted in ethnic exclusivity. To employ the 2,000 non-Serb police whom they have agreed to take, RS authorities would have to dismiss or reassign 1,500 current Serb officers, which has obvious political consequences for authorities as well as economic and social fallout for the dismissed and their families. The RS has also had a hard time wooing new officers from better-paid ranks in the Federation: according to 1998 estimates, Serb police earned only one-fifth the salary of their Federation counterparts.[38]

Efforts to depoliticize law enforcement and foster "multiethnic policing" can only go as far as Bosnia's structures of political authority.[39] It is worth recalling that Bosnian police, as in the former Yugoslavia, are managed through state ministries of the interior and are oriented toward internal security functions for the state more than policing for the population. Police command structure, budgets, and administration are tightly connected to governing authorities; indeed, the internal intelligence organs of the Bosniacs and Croats, which remain fully separate from one another, are often co-located with their respective local police.[40] The link between police and political leaderships was reinforced during the war, strengthened by the lack of an independent civil service, and unrestrained by Bosnia's less-than-independent, war-decimated judiciary.

Mixed Messages?

IPTF was asked to play an uncomfortably dual role of working supportively with local police while also keeping a watchful eye on them. On the one hand, their job was generally described as an "assistance program" to the parties' civilian law enforcement, including "advising law enforcement personnel and forces"; "training law enforcement personnel"; "facilitating, within the IPTF's mission of assistance, the Parties' law enforcement activities"; "assessing threats to public order"; and "assisting by accompanying the Parties' law enforcement personnel as they carry out their responsibilities."[41] On the other hand, IPTF was asked to monitor, observe, and inspect local law enforcement; "notify the High Representative and inform the IFOR Commander of failures to cooperate with the IPTF"; and provide any credible information about violations of human rights by law enforcement officials to Bosnia's Human Rights Commission *and* to the ICTY at The Hague.[42]

This tension persists in IPTF's work. Given its goal of building local police capacity, if also trying to reform it, IPTF's relationship naturally emphasizes assistance rather than inspection or investigation. IPTF has thus periodically found itself at odds with purpose-dedicated human rights offices, such as that within the Office of the High Representative.[43] The moral hazard, as one senior IPTF official put it, is that it had "tended to become advisers and capacity-builders instead of monitors and investigators," which risked "just training their thugs to be better thugs."[44]

In addition to this internal tension in its own mandate, IPTF has suffered from weaknesses typical of CIVPOL missions. The force depends entirely on contributions of personnel from member governments, and because domestic police are hard to disengage from their existing duties, the mission was understaffed for a prolonged initial period. What personnel IPTF received also often fell short of such minimum qualifications as years of experience, appropriate language ability, and driving skills, which was frequently discovered only after they were sent to Bosnia ("the number of those who failed to meet the criteria and to pass the required elementary tests upon arrival in theatre has risen to alarming levels").[45] At the end of March 1996, a mere 400 had arrived in theater, a full eighty of whom had to be returned to their governments.[46] Distinct from individual qualifications, police forces also vary widely among countries in norms of policing, which is to be expected, given that they hailed from more than thirty countries from Argentina through Nigeria to Ukraine.[47] This variety becomes a particular liability when a principal objective of their work is training, as has been IPTF's. Nor, as some might guess, was the greater weakness among police recruits from the developing world. Some of IPTF's earliest problems occurred with personnel from the United States and Canada, who initially tended to send retirees with less than vigorous enthusiasm for their job.[48] Recruits from France and Germany were problematic because they were fielded for only six months, a turnover rate that made it exceedingly difficult to build and maintain quality. Even had it started at full and fully qualified strength, however, a multilateral, unarmed police force is arguably an inappropriate vehicle for addressing the quasi- and paramilitary nature of policing in Bosnia, either to fill an enforcement gap or to reform state security forces.

Minding the Security Gap

During negotiations for the Dayton Agreement, Wesley Clark reportedly observed that between its military and police provisions, the agreement left "a huge gap in the Bosnia food chain."[49] Sadly, his insight has proved right. Especially in the first two years after the war ended, minority residents and opposition political figures were targets of systematic harassment and subject to what UNHCR characterized as a "climate of fear and intimidation."[50] Violence was often attributed to gangs or popular outbursts, but with negligible exceptions, most incidents clearly enjoyed the support of authorities and local security forces.[51] Hundreds of incidents worthy of public report occurred after Dayton's signing, most involving returning refugees or internally displaced persons, with every episode packing a double punch: the event itself and the fear that similar attacks would follow.[52]

The most dramatic episode occurred early, in March 1996, when the Serb-occupied Sarajevo suburbs were gutted and burned in the process of their transfer from Serb to Federation authority. During the month in which the five key suburbs were sequentially to be handed over, the situation deteriorated as nationalists on both sides intimidated or induced Serbs to vacate, dimming hopes for a multinational Sarajevo. The Pale Serb leadership launched what the UN called "an overt and insidious campaign of pressure to induce them [Serb residents] to leave," which included harassment, threatening visits from gangs, truck convoys to transport them from the city, destruction of all existing infrastructure ("hospitals clinics, schools, water, electricity and gas plants and factories were left completely stripped"), and arson. The Federation, meanwhile, gave Serbs little reassurance: Bosniac gangs intimidated Bosnian Serb residents, "robbing and looting their apartments in the process," and official television carried nothing but "religious and nationalist" programs throughout the period.[53]

As close to 60,000 Serbs fled, IFOR largely stood by, rejecting any involvement as "police work" and therefore outside its mandate.[54] IPTF was in no position to respond, even had the force been at full strength. As it was, they had 150 police monitors when the transfer of the suburbs began and only 350 when it concluded to try to create security for Serbs from both Bosniacs and the Serbs' own leadership.[55]

Primary responsibility for this "absence of ethnic security," as the International Crisis Group termed it, resided with local authorities, who were either directly involved (as in February 1997, when Croatian police in western Mostar fired into a crowd of unarmed Bosniac civilians attempting to visit a cemetery on a Muslim holiday, killing one and injuring twenty-seven) or indirectly involved (when local police have failed to protect civilians or their property when they were targeted by armed groups).[56] Police were also frequently involved in evictions of ethnic minorities.[57] International officials widely recognized where culpability lay. "Most of the violations of human rights which occur in Bosnia and Herzegovina (by some estimates as many as 70 percent) are the work of the police forces of the Entities themselves," reported the UN in late 1996. In 1997, the PIC Steering Board concluded that the "police not only frequently condone violence on ethnic and political grounds, they are often responsible for the violations themselves."[58]

Evidence that police were the primary abusers of human rights led the UN and others to argue that IPTF needed new authority to launch independent investigations of human rights abuses by Bosnian law enforcement officers. When the Peace Implementation Conference met in London in December 1996, it recommended that IPTF acquire new investigatory powers, which the UN Security Council authorized a week later when it extended IPTF's mandate for a year.[59] The role of the UN and IPTF in Bosnia has continued to evolve since then. They have increasingly emphasized police training over monitoring, which includes significant human rights components; the UN Mission in Bosnia and Herzegovina (UNMIBH) acquired a human rights unit of its own; and in 1998, UNMIBH launched an ambitious project to assess the needs of the Bosnian judicial system.[60]

The dilemmas for IPTF remain, however. It is required to be sufficiently close to Bosnian police to incline it to use those enforcement powers it has. The IPTF is also not able to structure, staff, or manage itself in such a way as to undertake the kind of serious, focused effort to build institutional capacity that Bosnia's police forces most need.

ASSESSMENT

Since the Dayton Agreement was signed, the military cease-fire in Bosnia has held firm. All armed forces have been reduced significantly in number, all operate with some degree of international oversight, and some progress has been made to integrate the Bosniac and Croat armies that together make up the Federation military. Notably, there have been no incidents of military-on-military violence or uses of force by one entity against the other, and those military provisions to which NATO leadership devoted their resources have been efficiently implemented according to the agreed-upon timetable. In addition, police and internal security forces have been drawn down significantly, a measure of their paramilitary capabilities have been reduced, and an impressive number on Federation and Serb sides have received human rights and other forms of training in international programs.

Unfortunately, joint ventures between the ABiH and HVO have gone no deeper than the surface, leaving both forces essentially separate. Each services its respective national leadership, with doctrine, capabilities, and intentions relatively opaque to one another and to the international community. There is even greater distance between them and the VRS. Thus, five years after Dayton, Bosnian territory remains clearly divided among the effective control of each of the country's three armies and related paramilitaries. As anxieties among international implementers grew about the viability of a peace based on even *two* armies within one country the NATO Secretary-General and Bosnia's

High Representative called for Bosnia to work toward a single, joint army. Even moderate Serbs rejected this appeal entirely.[61]

Moreover, this military control over territory translates directly into divided jurisdiction over public institutions and remains the central obstacle to building common institutions for a postwar Bosnian state. Worse, this division of spoils among Bosnia's forces was abetted by IFOR's and SFOR's early reliance upon a force separation strategy. IFOR and SFOR therefore missed a critical opportunity in failing to recognize early on the power of what Marcus Cox describes as "this nexus between armies and territory." With their mandated authority under Dayton, which empowers IFOR and SFOR to decide where armies deploy and from which areas they withdraw, both implementation forces had the power to sever the link between military control of territory and political jurisdiction; but they have so far failed to do so.[62]

The effective division of the country among three parallel security regimes has made it that much harder for implementers to contend with continuing violence and intimidation against ethnic minorities. From the Dayton Agreement's various provisions, one could infer an ambitious, even coherent commitment to public security. The parties were obliged to "provide a safe and secure environment for all persons living in their respective jurisdictions," ensure the "highest level" of effective respect for human rights, establish a "politically neutral environment," and "recreate as quickly as possible normal conditions of life in Bosnia and Herzegovina." IFOR, in turn, was authorized "to observe and prevent interference with the movement of civilian populations, refugees and displaced persons and to respond appropriately to deliberate violence to life and person." The parties also promised to conduct all law enforcement according to "internationally recognized standards and with respect for internationally recognized human rights and fundamental freedoms," in which they would be assisted by the IPTF. The problem was that deliberate violence to civilians was no less an effective instrument for political consolidation by the parties after the war than it was during it. Yet preventing this violence was a task neither wanted by IFOR, which was permitted but not obliged to undertake it, nor suitable for IPTF.

Beyond being a concern in its own right, the resultant gap has indirectly but powerfully affected other significant areas of implementation, such as return of refugees and internally displaced persons and the authenticity of elections. IFOR and subsequently SFOR, if to a lesser extent, have been rightly criticized for not embracing the full extent of their mandate. Only two years into the peace did they seriously focus on apprehending PIFWCs; protecting civilians from political violence, especially in the context of their return to their homes; creating a broader sense of security; or accomplishing important secondary tasks that were arguably critical to the political consolidation of peace in the country.

NOTES

1. GFAP, Annex I-A, Art. II/1, Art. III, Art. II/3.

2. IFOR actually included most UN troops who had been in Bosnia with UNPROFOR, who traded their light arms for heavy, and who repainted their white UN vehicles a military green. Richard C. Holbrooke, *To End a War* (New York: Random House, 1998), p. 324.

3. The ZOS posed a curious challenge to IFOR. Because it included the strip that followed the former line of confrontation, villages that lay within it were heavily damaged, if not completely destroyed. At the same time, because this area lay outside the control of either Serb or Federation authorities, it was conceivably more politically hospitable to the return of ethnic minorities. In late 1996, when a small number of Bosniacs tried unilaterally to return to their bombed-out homes, IFOR found itself in the perverse position of expelling them. See, for example, International Crisis Group, "Going Nowhere Fast: Refugees and Internally Displaced Persons in Bosnia," 30 April 1997.

4. According to the International Institute for Strategic Studies (IISS), *The Military Balance 1995/96* (London: Oxford University Press, 1995), levels in 1995 were as follows: ABiH, 92,000 active duty, 100,000 reserve; HVO, 50,000; VRS, 75,000; for a total of 319,000. U.S. sources put the wartime level as higher, at 410,000. See "Fact Sheet: Background on Bosnia and Herzegovina," *USIA Washington File* (Washington, DC: United States Information Agency, 1997). See also Arms Control section below.

5. There are clearly still pockets of mujahideen in central Bosnia, many of whom started families and then stayed when the war ended. See "Bosnian Muslims Protest Evictions," Radio Free Europe/Radio Liberty (RFE/RL) Newsline, 18 July 2000, describing a local state of emergency imposed near the town of Maglaj when several dozen Bosnians "of Middle East origin" protested their eviction to make room for Serb returnees.

6. Agreement on Sub-Regional Arms Control (Florence Agreement), 14 June 1996, negotiated under OSCE supervision. Available online at http://www.oscebih.org/downloads/regstab/art4-fin.pdf. The Florence Agreement, modeled on the Conventional Forces in Europe (CFE) Treaty, set ceilings on five categories of heavy weapons: battle tanks, armored combat vehicles, artillery 75 mm and larger, combat aircraft, and attack helicopters.

7. Stockholm International Peace Research Institute (SIPRI), *Yearbook 1998: Armaments, Disarmament and International Security* (New York: Oxford University Press, 1998), p. 519.

8. Different ratios were set for different categories of weaponry. Battle tanks, artillery, combat aircraft, and attack helicopters were set at a ratio of 2:1; ACVs at 1.9:1; and military personnel at 2.3:1. At this stage, the troop ceiling for the Federation as a whole was reduced to 45,000. SIPRI, *Yearbook 1998*, 519.

9. SIPRI, *Yearbook 1998,* 520. Significant confusion arose initially because of disparity between OSCE and IFOR/SFOR numbers, which derived from the difference in their approaches to counting—IFOR/SFOR "spot checks" versus OSCE's more systematic efforts. In August 1997, the organizations attempted to resolve this source of uncertainty through joint monitoring. SIPRI, *Yearbook 1998,* 518.

10. SIPRI, *Yearbook 1998,* 518.

11. Briefing on Train and Equip Program for the Bosnian Federation, Ambassador James W. Pardew, Jr., Special Representative for Military Stabilization in the Balkans, 24 July 1996. Available online at http://www.state.gov/www/regions/eur/bosnia/724brief_bosnia_federation.htm.

12. Ibid.

13. Ibid. Also IISS, *The Military Balance 1997/98,* 77.

14. One of the more surprising supporters of train and equip has been the independent International Crisis Group. Even as they acknowledged the program's risks, their position was that the policy could foster confidence building, transparency, and even integration, especially if the emphasis was on "training" more than "equipping." See International Crisis Group, "A Peace or Just a Cease-fire? The Military Equation in Post-Dayton Bosnia," 15 December 1997, pp. 5–13.

15. MPRI won the contract after a competitive bidding process with other U.S. contractors. See David Isenberg, "Soldiers of Fortune Ltd.: A Profile of Today's Private Sector Corporate Mercenary Firms," p. 14. Available online at http://www.cdi.org/isssues/mercenaries/merc1.html.

16. Involved countries include Turkey, Saudi Arabia, Kuwait, the United Arab Emirates, Malaysia, and Brunei.

17. See, for example, Jane M. O. Sharp, "Dayton Report Card," *International Security* 22, no. 3 (winter 1997–1998): 116; and Holbrooke, *To End a War,* 276–280.

18. Holbrooke, *To End a War,* 277.

19. Sharp, "Dayton Report Card," 116. In the words of one senior civilian official in August 1998, "You could measure the time it takes for fighting to break out after NATO leaves in nano-seconds." Author interview, Sarajevo.

20. Confidential interviews, SFOR, UNMIBH, Sarajevo, August 1998.

21. International Crisis Group, *Is Dayton Failing? Bosnia Four Years After the Peace Agreement* (Brussels, Belgium: 1999), p. 29.

22. SIPRI, *Yearbook 1999,* 634.

23. Confidential interview, SFOR, Sarajevo, August 1998.

24. We are grateful to Marcus Cox for this point.

25. A variety of factors prompted the shift in international policy, including a changing of the foreign policy guard in major capitals and institutions: Tony Blair had become UK prime minister, bringing with him a new foreign policy team; Madeleine Albright was the new U.S. secretary of state; Wesley Clark replaced George Joulwan as NATO Supreme Allied Commander in Europe; not least, the U.S. presidential election was safely past.

26. SFOR troops also seized several radio and television transmitters in the summer of 1997 because of Serb broadcasts that seemed designed to incite violence, particularly against SFOR and other international personnel.

27. The two were picked up in Prijedor. For detail about the arrest, see *Tribunal Update 36: Last Week in The Hague (July 7–12, 1997).* For coverage

of Prijedor's politics, see also Human Rights Watch/Helsinki Report, "The Unindicted: Reaping the Rewards of 'Ethnic Cleansing,'" January 1997.

28. International Criminal Tribunal for Yugoslavia, see articles online at http://www.un.org/icty/glance/detainees-e.htm.

29. A UN advance team in December 1995 estimated that Bosnian police numbered 45,000 in all, with 12,000 Serbs, 29,750 Bosniacs, and 3,000 Croats. On this basis, the UN Secretary-General recommended an initial IPTF strength of 1,721 (S/1995/1031, 13 December 1995), subsequently authorized under Security Council Resolution 1035 (13 December 1995). Of course, the same advance team recommended a force structure in which IPTF would deploy in teams to each of Bosnia's 109 municipalities, a recommendation that the first IPTF commissioner found "operationally unnecessary, administratively complicated and therefore not advisable" once he saw conditions on the ground for himself. See S/1996/210 (29 March 1996), par. 7.

30. Annex 11, Art. II. Through the end of 1995, it was thought that the UN civil affairs officers already on the ground with UNPROFOR might be put at the service of the new High Representative. Instead, the UN retained a Special Representative of the Secretary-General under a new UN Mission in Bosnia and Herzegovina, under which the IPTF operates. Confidential interview, OHR and UNMIBH, Sarajevo, November 1996. See also "Report of the Secretary-General," S/1995/1031, par. 38, and Press Release SC/6150, par. 3.

31. "The IPTF Commissioner or his or her representatives *may* attend meetings of the Joint Civilian Commission established in Annex 10 . . . and of the Joint Military Commission established in Annex 1"; "The IPTF Commissioner *may* request that meetings of appropriate commissions be convened to discuss issues." Emphasis added, Annex 11, Art. II, par. 8.

32. Confidential interview, IPTF, November 1996. Since 1999, IPTF numbers have fallen below authorized levels because of demands for UN civilian police elsewhere, especially in Kosovo. In June 2000, IPTF numbered 1,602 ("Report of the Secretary-General on the United Nations Mission in Bosnia and Herzegovina," S/2000/529, 1).

33. Confidential interview, IPTF, Sarajevo, August 1998.

34. ICG, *Is Dayton Failing?* 115.

35. Ibid., 113, 111. The Federation benchmark was set by an Agreement on Restructuring the Police Federation, 25 April 1996 (the "Bonn-Petersburg Agreement"); the RS level was agreed between UNMIBH and the RS Ministry of the Interior in a Framework Agreement on Police Restructuring Reform and Democratization in Republika Srpska, 9 December 1998.

36. By 1999, rates of completed training in human dignity were 94 percent in the Federation and 99 percent in the RS; rates for transitional training were 79 percent in the Federation and 38.5 percent in the RS. ICG, *Is Dayton Failing?* 112, 114.

37. ICG, *Is Dayton Failing?* 116. The greatest resistance over arm patches has occurred in hard-line Croat areas, such as Drvar.

38. The salary for Serbs is DM 80, compared to DM 400. ICG, *Is Dayton Failing?* 111.

39. Charles Call has made this point more broadly, that security sector reform is constrained by the existing "political geography" in a given society.

40. According to ICG, the Bosnian Croat intelligence is integrally tied to Croatian state intelligence. ICG, *Is Dayton Failing?* 115.

41. GFAP, Annex 11, Art. III.

42. GFAP, Annex 11, Art. V–VI.

43. One example is the Vasic case. In early 1998, Federation police apprehended a Serb in the ZOS for alleged war crimes, breaking two major procedural rules in the process: they used long-barreled weapons, which police were forbidden to carry; and they broke the "Rules of the Road Procedures" agreed to in Rome on 18 February 1996, which guaranteed that individuals not subject to an ICTY indictment could only be apprehended if pursuant to a previously issued domestic order, warrant, or indictment that had been reviewed and approved by the ICTY. IPTF saw this as an act that they should encourage Federation authorities to investigate and judge through their own processes, especially since the existing chief of police in Sarajevo was seen as relatively pro-reform. Contrarily, OHR—Principal Deputy Jacques Paul Klein, in particular—pushed hard for international sanctions, specifically that the minister of the interior and the Sarajevo chief of police should be fired. Notably, this incident took place at a time when the United States was actively supporting the moderate Serb leader Milorad Dodik and trying harder to establish its Serb-friendly credentials. Confidential interview, IPTF, Sarajevo, March 1998.

44. Confidential interview, UNMIBH, Sarajevo, August 1998.

45. "Report of the Secretary General," S/1996/210 (29 March 1996), par. 8.

46. Ibid.

47. The list of countries contributing CIVPOL to Bosnia has varied somewhat. Lists of countries and their police contributions are listed in the quarterly reports of the Secretary-General to the Security Council pursuant to the Council's Resolutions 1035 and 1088, respectively.

48. Confidential interview, IPTF, Sarajevo, November 1996. In 1997, Canada began sending Royal Mounted Police to IPTF, and standards rose perceptibly. Confidential interviews, IPTF, Sarajevo, August 1998.

49. Quoted in Holbrooke, *To End a War,* 252.

50. UNHCR, Humanitarian Issues Working Group, "Bosnia and Herzegovina: Repatriation and Return Operation 1997," UN Document HIWG/97/2, Geneva, 23 April 1997, par. 40.

51. Agence France Presse, Reuters, and RFE/RL Newsline, 1996 to present. Confidential interviews, UNMIBH, IPTF, and OHR, 1996 to present.

52. Author's count based on reports by IPTF, UN Civil Affairs, the International Crisis Group, and newswires.

53. "Report of the Secretary-General," S/1996/210, pars. 32–35.

54. See Dan De Luce, "Fires Burn in Lawless Sarajevo Suburb," *Reuters European Community Report,* 9 March 1996; and Chris Hedges, "Sarajevo District Burns," *New York Times,* 18 March 1996, p. A6. See also UNHCR, Executive Committee of the High Commissioner's Programme, "Update on Regional Developments in the Former Yugoslavia," UN Document EC/47/SC/CRP.18 (9 April 1997), par. 3.

55. "Report of the Secretary-General," S/1996/210, par. 35. "I must stress that annex 11 to the Peace Agreement envisages the Task Force as an unarmed, monitoring and advisory force," the Secretary-General argued in an early report to the Security Council. "It is not feasible to assign to this unarmed force the task of enforcing law and order in a country awash with weapons, all the more so when it has no legal authority to do so" (par. 42).

56. Chris Bennett, author interview, Sarajevo, November 1996.

57. IPTF briefing for author, Banja Luka, November 1996.

58. Conclusions reached at Sintra, UN Document S/1997/434 (5 June 1997), par. 55. UN Document S/1996/1017 (9 December 1996), par. 15.

59. Conclusions of the Peace Implementation Conference, S/1996/1012 (6 December 1996), par. 77. The authorization was made in Security Council Res. 1088 (12 December 1996), par. 28; this resolution also authorized SFOR for a period of eighteen months.

60. S/Res/1168 (21 May 1998) authorized UNMIBH to conduct a "court monitoring" program to supplement the UN's police work and OHR's legal reform efforts. This program was subsequently discontinued when U.S. congressional funding was cut. See note 30 for more information on UNMIBH.

61. See RFE/RL Newsline (18 July 2000).

62. Marcus Cox, correspondence with author, 10 October 2000.

4

Refugees and
Internally Displaced Persons

Bosnia's war was propelled significantly by competing nationalist claims to Bosnian territory. As the Yugoslav state disintegrated, the status of Bosnian Serbs and Croatians within an independent Bosnia was put in doubt, given a Muslim majority and the dominance of the Muslim-led SDA. Anticipating a loss of status, nationalist leaderships among both communities and their respective patrons in Belgrade and Zagreb effectively launched a civil war as a preemptive strike against the prospect of a Muslim Bosnia. Their goal was "ethnic cleansing" of territory that could later be incorporated into Serbia or Croatia, and their primary tactic was forced migration. At the war's end, there were more than 1.2 million refugees and 1 million internally displaced persons (IDPs)—out of a prewar population of merely 4.4 million Bosnians.[1] A staggering one-half of the country's people were forcibly displaced during the conflict.[2]

The Dayton Agreement and its implementation proposed to reverse the effects of this deliberate mass displacement. The principal challenge, beyond the extraordinary logistical one, was that nationalist politicians on all sides remained in power, arguably strengthened and unlikely to allow a remixing of populations that would dilute their political power. Further complicating the situation, there were also serious tensions among international actors regarding how best to promote multiethnicity and to what extent this goal should be given primacy in international implementation efforts.

In its Agreement on Refugees and Displaced Persons (Annex 7), the Dayton Agreement stipulated an unqualified right of return: "All refugees and displaced persons have the right to freely return to their homes of origin. They shall have the right to have restored to them property of which they were deprived in the course of hostilities since

71

1991 and to be compensated for any property that can not be restored to them."[3]

The accord set a precedent as well as an extremely high benchmark for success by guaranteeing a right of return not to a displaced person's country but to his or her "home of origin," a level of specificity that could be said to extend beyond existing standards or practices for the rights of the displaced.[4] Dayton also obligated the signatories to create the conditions necessary for peaceful repatriation and reintegration, including a commitment to a range of "confidence building measures."[5] In its Agreement on Human Rights (Annex 6), moreover, Dayton committed the Bosnian parties to a comprehensive range of international human rights and humanitarian standards, including the 1951 Convention Relating to the Status of Refugees and its accompanying 1966 Protocol.[6]

Lead responsibility for ensuring Dayton's right of return was assigned to the UNHCR, whose primary tasks were to plan, coordinate, and implement refugee repatriation and IDP return. In the process, the agency also took on a wide range of related activities that involved additional agencies and NGOs, such as providing temporary and permanent housing, tracing missing persons, providing medical assistance, distributing food, and protecting those who had been displaced. Over time, the OHR has also assumed return-related functions, largely in policy development and coordination, through the creation of a Reconstruction and Return Task Force (RRTF) in January 1997.

REFUGEE REPATRIATION

After nearly four years of war, approximately 1.2 million people had fled Bosnia to host countries, where they resided as refugees.[7] The exact composition and patterns of displacement among Bosnia's refugees is the subject of highly politicized debate, but general lines are fairly clear. Bosniacs constituted a heavy majority of the refugee population, originating primarily from Serb-dominated eastern Bosnia (now Republika Srpska) and secondarily from Croat areas, and found refuge mostly in European countries outside the Balkans. Ethnic Croats fled mostly to Croatia, having been forced from Serb-held territory and to a lesser extent from Bosniac areas. Ethnic Serbs were expelled from Bosniac and Croat territories that now comprise the Federation and went primarily to the FRY.[8] At the end of the war, about 685,000 refugees were living in western Europe—including approximately

330,000 in Germany alone;[9] and 446,500 were distributed among Yugoslavia's former republics (250,000 in the FRY; 170,000 in Croatia; 16,500 Bosnians in Slovenia; and 10,000 Bosnians in Macedonia).[10]

Initially UNHCR and other implementers emphasized repatriation to areas where the displaced could be assured of their security. With IFOR's troop-contributing states unwilling to see the force used assertively to provide security for ethnic minorities and without a credible alternative to ensure public security, UNHCR was put in an exceedingly difficult position. The agency had little choice but to give priority to repatriation in areas where refugees belonged to the ethnic majority. The security environment also dictated the lesser attention given initially to internally displaced persons who, by definition, would primarily be minority returnees. The irony, of course, was that the relative impossibility of return to homes of origin meant that refugees would, in effect, be repatriating to a condition of internal displacement. Sadako Ogata, the UN High Commissioner for Refugees, made this point clear to the Peace Implementation Conference in December 1995: "Given the traumas of the past and possible apprehension for the future, many people may, at least initially, prefer to return to their majority Entity. Their wish should be fully respected. Whereas ethnic depopulation was an objective of some parties during the war, ethnic repopulation should not become an objective during peace."[11] This emphasis on repatriation to majority areas persisted throughout the first year of Dayton implementation, until the tension between this approach and the simultaneous objective of reintegration grew publicly insupportable.

Even with majority return as a priority, the results of implementation disappointed early projections. UNHCR anticipated the return of as many as 400,000 Bosnian refugees in 1996 in a combination of organized, assisted, and spontaneous return, yet only 88,039 refugees actually repatriated during that year.[12] Subsequent years yielded similarly modest numbers: 120,280 refugees returned in 1997; 110,000 in 1998; and 31,650 in 1999; for a total of 349,969 over four years (see Table 4.1).[13]

Table 4.1   Refugee Repatriation to Bosnia, 1996–1999

	Postwar	1996	1997	1998	1999	Total
Refugees[a]	1,200,000	1,025,000	612,000	424,000	324,100	NA
Repatriation	NA	88,039	120,280	110,000	31,650	349,969

Sources: Various years and documents from UNHCR, ICG, and USCR.
Note: a. "Refugees" refers to those still in need of a durable solution.

Overwhelmingly, repatriation has meant the return of refugees to areas where they are in the ethnic majority. Between 1996 and 1999, only 12,078 Serbs repatriated to Federation territory, and a bare 3,233 Bosniacs and Croats repatriated to Republika Srpska.[14] In contrast, more than 310,000 Bosniacs and Croat refugees moved back to the Federation, and more than 20,000 Serbs returned to Republika Srpska during the same time period, dramatically reinforcing the postwar trend to consolidate ethnicity rather than diversify it.[15] Furthermore, although a drop-off in returns during 1999 can be at least partly attributed to regional insecurity stemming from the Kosovo conflict, it also indicates that most of what some have called "easy cases"—voluntary return to majority areas—have already been accomplished and that most of those remaining abroad after 1998 constitute much harder cases of reluctant minority returns.[16]

Independent of the question of majority versus minority returns, international efforts had managed to return less than one-third of Bosnia's original pool of wartime refugees by early 2000. Estimates are that approximately 324,000 Bosnian refugees remained without a durable solution in November 1999, and close to one half of the initial refugee population had found durable solutions abroad such as political asylum, third-country resettlement, or citizenship.[17] By the end of 1997, 504,000 Bosnians had reportedly found durable solutions outside the country. Of these, about 110,000 resettled in Canada or the United States, nearly 180,000 were given citizenship in Croatia, and approximately 210,000 refugees attained long-term status in other countries throughout western Europe.[18] Permanent third-country resettlement of refugees has continued as a trend, if at lower numbers.[19]

RETURN OF INTERNALLY DISPLACED PERSONS

By most estimates, the Bosnian war displaced at least 1 million people from their "home of origin" to temporary residence elsewhere within Bosnian territory. In the immediate aftermath of the war, a significant number of internally displaced persons lived in collective centers, either internationally funded and administered or maintained by domestic revenue and personnel. In early 1996, UNHCR and partner organizations were funding or administrating 321 centers throughout Bosnia, which accommodated close to 50,000 IDPs.[20]

Many more IDPs had taken refuge in housing formerly occupied by other Bosnians who had fled, either as refugees or as internally displaced persons. Bosniacs and Bosnian Croats expelled from what became Republika Srpska occupied housing abandoned by Serbs who had been forced to leave what would subsequently become the Federation; Bosnian Serbs forced to leave what became Federation territory occupied housing previously inhabited by Bosniacs and Bosnian Croats; and Bosniacs and Bosnian Croats, in turn, squatted in one another's housing within the Federation.

The initial international approach to IDP return mirrored that for refugees and was conditioned by the adequacy of security and, secondarily, housing and prospects for employment. Since IDPs had, by definition, been displaced because they were not welcome elsewhere in the country, this stance really only restated the problem: namely, that a war had been fought to cleanse minorities into majority areas, and an implementation effort was under way to reverse precisely that. In the absence of guarantees by IFOR or a broader strategy to create conditions in which Bosnia could be ethnically reintegrated, international efforts in the first years of Dayton implementation roughly amounted to rhetorical appeals for multiethnicity without an effectively concerted effort among implementers, donors, and supportive governments to realize it.

IDP return has been both modest in its numbers and complex in its dynamics. The biggest year for IDP return was 1996, when 164,741 Bosnians moved back to their home of origin.[21] Subsequent years yielded even slimmer results: 58,295 in 1997; 29,570 in 1998; and 43,385 in 1999; for a total of 295,991, or just under one-third of the total wartime pool (see Table 4.2).[22] Although this number is not negligible, it is further qualified by the fact that additional internal displacements occurred after the war ended. The most prominent instance of postwar displacement occurred when 60,000 Serbs fled from Sarajevo's suburbs during their transfer from Serb occupation to Federation control, leaving only 8,000 Bosnian Serbs remaining in an SDA-dominated Sarajevo.[23] Many other smaller incidents, cumulatively, have taken an analogous toll. As a result, even though 295,991 IDPs returned, the pool of those still considered internally displaced at the end of 1999 was not 700,000, as one might expect, but approximately 830,000.

Table 4.2   IDP Returns Within Bosnia, 1996–1999

	Postwar	1996	1997	1998	1999	Total
IDP[a]	1,000,000	874,295	816,000	836,000	830,000	NA
Returns	NA	164,741	58,295	29,570	43,385	295,991

Sources: Various years and documents from UNHCR, ICG, and USCR.
Note: a. IDP also reflects relocation during each year.

Additional factors have been at work. Not all IDPs have actually sought to return to original homes. For many, to do so entails confronting security risks and frail prospects for jobs or social welfare. For others, return may even represent a step backward. Among rural Bosniacs who fled to Sarajevo, for instance, a return to stagnant village life is not an appealing prospect.[24] To complicate the statistical picture, significant numbers of refugees have repatriated to areas where they would be among an ethnic majority.[25] Are these to be considered successfully returned refugees, new additions to the ranks of internally displaced, or both? Rather than reversing wartime demographic patterns of ethnic cleansing, then, most postwar IDP movements have been majority returns that have had the effect of consolidating ethnic homogeneity.

MINORITY RETURNS

The question of "minority return" lies at the heart of Dayton's return provisions, even though it did not become a practical priority among implementers until 1997. The experience with minority return and sequential international efforts to advance it highlight the unavoidable interdependence among major arenas of implementation: in particular, security as guaranteed by IFOR, SFOR, and IPTF; reconstruction as spearheaded by the World Bank and bilateral donors; and political reform as sought by the PIC and OHR.

From the beginning, the absence of freedom of movement militated against minority return. Although the Dayton Agreement, including Bosnia's new constitution, guaranteed a "right to liberty of movement and residence," this was a difficult right to enforce in the aftermath of the war, even for those displaced persons who merely wished to conduct assessment visits to see the condition of their former homes before trying to return to them. Freedom of movement was restricted by a maze of illegal police checkpoints and rumors of long "lists" of Hague indictees who could be apprehended without due process; illicit tolls at interentity crossing points; the scattering of 600,000 active landmines throughout Bosnia, particularly along the IEBL; and actual violence in the form of attacks on individuals and small groups of travelers.[26] These last were often reported as spontaneous acts by "mobs" but in almost all cases were shown to have been organized by political authorities. In April 1996, for example, close to 100 Serbs attacked a Muslim convoy of about 250 IDPs returning to their former homes in Trnovo, south of Sarajevo, despite the presence of an IFOR escort.[27] In May 1998, a Bosniac crowd prevented a bus with about fifty Serb IDPs from visiting their former village of Sanica in the Federation by throwing stones, seriously injuring an elderly woman.[28]

To offset restricted movement among displaced minorities, UNHCR introduced at the outset of implementation an interentity bus service that greatly facilitated travel between the Federation and Republika Srpska. By 1997, the bus service had transported 460,000 Bosnians across the IEBL—an average of nearly 9,000 people per week.[29] Gradually, other implementation efforts also helped promote greater freedom of movement. The International Police Task Force has steadily tried to reduce the general level of harassment by local police and, by mid-1997, had finally succeeded in removing illegal checkpoints. SFOR has also shown greater willingness than IFOR to extend its security umbrella over civilian population movements. Thanks to creativity within UN Civil Affairs and OHR, a common license plate for civilian vehicles was introduced in mid-1998, which allowed Bosnians to travel throughout the country without revealing their ethnicity on their vehicles' license plate.[30]

Over time, it became increasingly clear that minority return depended upon active coordination between major components of the larger implementation effort. One of the earliest attempts at IDP return was UNHCR's Pilot Return Project, designed to swap Bosniac and Croat IDPs within the Federation. Stemming from an agreement brokered on the sidelines of the Dayton negotiations, this initiative was intended to be a reciprocal exchange of displaced populations among four towns in the Federation to be completed by December 1995. According to the plan, the Croat-controlled towns of Stolac and Jajce would receive 100 and 200 Bosniac families, respectively, and the Bosniac-controlled towns of Travnik and Bugojno would receive 100 and 200 Croat families, respectively. Travnik was fairly receptive to Croat returnees, but Bugojno's leaders openly obstructed Croat returns, and the agreed-upon returns did not take place. The situation was far worse in the Croat towns of Jajce and Stolac. Despite initial openness in Jajce, acts of violence and arson prompted 400–500 Muslim returnees to flee in mid-1997; only after British SFOR troops escorted the Bosniacs to Jajce directly were they allowed to stay.[31] And Stolac was so persistently resistant that Bosniacs had not returned to any significant extent by 2000.

Meanwhile, in collaboration with major donor governments, UNHCR launched its Open Cities Initiative (OCI) in March 1997. The OCI relied upon positive conditionality, rewarding those municipalities receptive to minority returns with increased donor funds. In brief, UNHCR's criteria for designation as an Open City were the following: (1) genuine and consistent political will demonstrated by the local authorities after publicly declaring their cities to be Open Cities; (2) confirmation that minority returns were occurring or would take place without any abuse of these minorities; (3) and confirmation that local authorities were genuinely committed to consistent and equal support for all members of the population for which they were responsible.[32]

By mid-1999, the distribution of UNHCR Open Cities was as follows: four in Republika Srpska (Mrkonjic Grad, Sipovo, Laktasi, and Srbac) and eleven in the Federation (Ilijas, Konjic, Busovaca, Bihac, Gorazde, Kakanj, Zenica, Ilidza, Zavidovici, Tuzla, and Travnik).[33] Only one Open City—Vogosca municipality in the Sarajevo Canton—has been "de-recognised" for a "lack of co-operation and unwillingness to meet the benchmarks set by UNHCR."[34]

Although OCI may have brought some benefits to participating municipalities, its record has been mixed. Opponents have offered a range of criticisms, including the following: UNHCR's administration of the program was both timid and unfocused because of tensions between OCI's use of conditionality and UNHCR's traditional stance of neutrality among parties; selection criteria for participating cities have been neither transparent nor consistently applied; city leaders have needed to show only the most superficial commitment in order to continue receiving funding; political conditionality has adversely affected cities excluded from the program; and majority returns, attracted by the economic opportunities, have actually outnumbered minority returns in most OCI sites—thus defeating the stated purpose of the program to shift ethnic demographics toward diversity. The bottom line is that OCI has not brought about minority returns at the level one would expect, given the amount of scarce resources expended.

Finally, there were also coordination problems between UNHCR and major donors. The United States, for instance, dissatisfied with the pace of OCI's administration, began unilaterally recognizing and funding municipalities that it considered open to minority returns. When questioned on this issue, the U.S. director of the program responded: "We don't call this the 'Open Cities Initiative' anymore because this is unilateral. We control the project. We call it 'Special Assistance for Communities that Express an Openness for Minority Return.'"[35]

In recognition that greater coherence was needed among international efforts, OHR and UNHCR formed the RRTF in January 1997 to serve as an interagency forum for the planning and coordination of return-related efforts. The RRTF has since developed a series of action plans designed to remedy the perceived failures of various earlier initiatives. The RRTF's 1999 strategy, for example, revolved around five key elements: locating return axes, following the flow of returns, negotiating "beachhead" returns, identifying security risks, and improving information management.[36] The RRTF subsequently turned to explicit efforts to depoliticize the minority return process. Under the auspices of the Property Law Implementation Plan (PLIP), first conceived in October 1999, the RRTF began to focus on consistent enforcement of individual rights rather than brokering group returns of displaced persons.[37] This tack has had a positive impact, and voluntary compliance with property laws is now increasing among Bosnians—thus improving the prospects for minority returns in aggregate.

However, on balance, the return of minority refugees and internally displaced persons has been less than anticipated by international actors (see Table 4.3). Early efforts yielded minimal results on minority returns to Republika Srpska. RS receptivity to minority returns increased in 1998 and 1999 but was still far below international expectations. In sum, only 24,103 Bosniacs and Croats returned to their homes in Republika Srpska during the first four years of Dayton implementation. The situation has been only marginally better with regard to Serbs returning to the Federation. A total of 35,324 Serbs managed to return to the Federation through early 2000, only slightly more than half the number who had fled post-Dayton Sarajevo during the handover to Federation authorities. Perhaps unsurprisingly, the greatest number of minority returns occurred between Bosniac and Croat areas within the Federation—the total of 69,340 represents more than half the entire country's 128,767 minority returns from 1996 to 1999. During the first five months of 2000, notably, prospects for minority return appeared to be improving significantly, with the total number of registered minority returns at three times the level during the same period in 1999.[38]

Table 4.3 Minority Returns to and Within Bosnia, 1996–1999

	1996	1997	1998	1999	Total
Republika Srpska:					
Bosniac and Croat Minority Returns	1,096	1,123	8,592	13,292	24,103
Federation:					
Serb Minority Returns	1,785	6,691	12,119	14,729	35,324
Federation:					
Bosniac and Croat Minority Returns	8,785	26,023	20,564	13,968	69,340
BiH:					
Total	11,666	33,837	41,275	41,989	128,767

Sources: Various years and documents from UNHCR, ICG, and USCR.

LEGAL AND SOCIAL BARRIERS TO RETURN

The Dayton Agreement anticipated that establishing legal ownership of residential property would be a central challenge to prospects for return, and it called for creation of a commission to handle competing claims. According to Annex 7, this Commission for Real Property Claims of Displaced Persons and Refugees would not "recognize as valid any illegal property transaction, including any transfer that was made under duress, in exchange for exit permission or documents, or that was otherwise in connection with ethnic cleansing."[39] Dayton authorized the CRPC to hear and decide claims to property that was alleged to have involuntarily changed ownership or occupancy during the war (since 1 April 1992).

According to a 1999 survey conducted by the CRPC of nearly 3,000 persons displaced within Bosnia or as refugees in Croatia and FRY, 61 percent of all respondents indicated a desire to return to their home of origin, whereas 38 percent preferred to sell, lease, or exchange their property. Bosniac and Croat IDPs desired to return home the most, by 76 percent and 73 percent, respectively, but only 36 percent of Serb IDPs showed an inclination to return to their prewar location. Of those who preferred not to return, the following were the most important factors influencing their preference: security, unfamiliar neighbors, employment prospects, the prospect of no longer being in the ethnic majority, and a lack of family in the area. According to all respondents, the following factors were the most important in determining whether to return, remain abroad, or relocate: neighbors of same ethnic group, trust in local authorities, employment opportunities, schools for children, and quality of housing.[40]

Prior to the war, 80 percent of housing in Bosnia was privately held (mostly in rural areas), and 20 percent was socially owned (mostly in urban areas).[41] While physical reconstruction of the housing stock in Bosnia has proceeded at a reasonable pace, establishing postwar ownership and occupancy rights for housing throughout the country has remained a challenge. Both RS and Federation parliaments initially imposed legislative roadblocks to deter returnees from reclaiming prewar property. Under intense pressure from the Peace Implementation Council and OHR, both the Federation (April 1998) and Republika Srpska (December 1998) either repealed or amended these property laws to conform to the principles outlined under Dayton and also set up new municipal structures to handle property claims.

Whether such legal reforms have been properly implemented is another question. By the end of 1998, CRPC had received 148,167 property claims but had only been able to decide on one-sixth of these.[42] This result was no great surprise, given that CRPC was chronically understaffed and underfunded, which OHR has frequently lobbied to try to change. As of September 1999, the record of the municipal offices established by the Bosnian government to handle claims was even worse: of 85,000 claims registered in the Federation, only 12,000 had received decisions, eventually resulting in 3,000 reinstatements; of the 38,000 claims registered in Republika Srpska, only 3,000 had received decisions, eventually resulting in 600 reinstatements.[43] Over time, both the CRPC and municipal offices increased their productivity. As of June 2000, out of the 225,000 property claims registered by the CRPC and municipal offices in Bosnia, 35 percent of claimants have had their status as owners confirmed, and 13 percent of claimants have physically regained possession of their homes.[44]

Lack of employment prospects has exerted a further dampening effect on return, both majority and minority. Unemployment remains high and has been significantly worse among returnees, especially minorities. In fact, competition for jobs has been so fierce that even majority returnees experienced resentment from co-nationals whose job security may be equally precarious. This powerful link between economic prospects and community receptiveness to return, both majoritarian and minority, was insufficiently appreciated in the early period of Dayton implementation. Instead, the early withholding of international reconstruction assistance from Serb areas, largely to refrain from bolstering ICTY indictees and nationalists, had a perverse effect by perpetuating high unemployment in precisely the areas that were considered priorities for minority return.

Bosnians' concern about "trust in local authorities" also reflected the nearly unchecked power of municipal leaders over the distribution of a wide range of social benefits and community services, from access to humanitarian assistance to medical care, education, and pensions. Bureaucratic roadblocks against returnees have been common, such as municipal authorities' requiring unattainable forms of identification in order to register for local assistance, and have been directed particularly at ethnic minorities throughout Bosnia.[45] Finally, appropriate access to education for children, identified as a majority priority by displaced Bosnians in the CRPC survey, has been difficult to attain. For years, Bosniacs, Croats, and Serbs have maintained three different curricula, strongly discouraged minority enrollment, and continued to resist efforts such as OHR's to develop a more inclusive and integrated system. The obvious implication for potential minority returns is that they will have to educate their children elsewhere. Although each such obstacle—housing, employment, social welfare, or education—may not have been insurmountable on its own, cumulatively they posed a substantial impediment to return.

ASSESSMENT

Bosnia's ruling parties have shown themselves adept at developing numerous instruments of resistance to the repatriation and return of the displaced. Many of their tactics represent clear "out-group" coercion, or intimidation and violence used by one ethnic group against displaced persons from another. Other tactics, however, reflect use of "in-group" coercion, or intimidation by a nationalist leadership against its own constituency. Gojko Klickovic, the head of Bosnian Serb resettlement, typified this type of intimidation when he reportedly remarked, "We must not allow a single Serb to remain in the territories which fall under Muslim-Croat control."[46] Also, it should be noted that some forms of resistance to return efforts, whether in-group or out-group, have been less overt. For example, the numerous difficulties that minorities in Bosnia have had in obtaining social welfare, medical care, identity documents, pensions, and the resolution of their housing situation are indicative of a more subtle form of obstruction designed to discourage displaced persons from returning to their homes of origin.

Although resistance to return can take many forms, international implementers primarily focused on combating overt forms of out-group coercion, with insufficient recognition of the limits of this approach or the potency of in-group coercion and more subtle forms of obstruction. For example, the use of political conditionality on donor aid was designed to remedy out-group coercion but arguably strengthened the hold of nationalist politicians because it fails to recognize the power of in-group dynamics. A comprehensive return strategy would go beyond the more visible out-group coercion to address the incentives and pressures used by ruling parties among their own co-nationals. Finally, international use of political conditionality, whether "carrots" (e.g., Open Cities Initiative) or "sticks" (e.g., denial of aid to Republika Srpska during 1996 and 1997), has had marginal utility when dealing with social relations among Bosnians and more subtle, bureaucratic forms of obstruction to integration such as the denial of social welfare benefits or delays processing a housing claim.

The challenges of Dayton implementation, over time, have compelled international implementers to approach refugee and IDP return in new ways. What might conventionally have been treated as a humanitarian concern was clearly central to the larger process of state building envisioned at Dayton, in which international actors were centrally implicated. The operational implications were multiple. Return would be resisted politically, administratively, and even paramilitarily by the parties, requiring an integration of humanitarian and security assistance that was unprecedented; it was also heavily interdependent with economic reconstruction and development. In the years after 1995, implementers made gradual progress in bringing their own efforts to bear more coherently on the return question. International actors learned from the counterproductive inconsistency of initial approaches (such as Pilot Return Projects and the Open Cities Initiative), and thus the current RRTF policy, focused on the more technical problem of an even application of the rule of law, began to pay dividends for Bosnia's displaced persons.

Although debates within the international community regarding the merits of promoting minority returns versus majority relocation have been essentially resolved by emphasizing the *centrality of choice* for individual displaced persons, work also remains to be done to promote Bosnian social, economic, and political parameters that would facilitate realization of this right in practice. Thus, four years after Dayton, there were still approximately 324,000 Bosnian refugees and 830,000 IDPs in need of a durable solution.[47] Finding a consensual and expeditious resolution of their plight, whether return or relocation, remains a challenge for both Bosnians and the international community.

NOTES

1. These numbers are most often cited, thought there is some variation among reputable sources: for example, ICG puts the number of refugees at 1.3 million ("Minority Return or Mass Relocation?" 14 May 1998, footnote 12), and early UNHCR estimates put the IDP population in December 1995 at closer to 1.1 million (UNHCR, *Refugees and Others of Concern to UNHCR: 1996 Statistical Overview*, table 2, p. 15).

2. We use the general term *displaced person* when there is no need to distinguish between refugees and internally displaced.

3. General Framework Agreement for Peace in Bosnia and Herzegovina, Annex 7, Art. I, par. 1.

4. Howard Adelman, "Peace Agreements: Refugee Repatriation and Reintegration," in Stephen John Stedman, Donald Rothchild, and Elizabeth M. Cousens, eds., "Strategies, Organizations, and Consequences: Explaining the Outcome of Peace Implementation in Civil Wars," vol. 2 of "Ending Civil Wars," a joint research project of the Center for International Security and Cooperation and the International Peace Academy, unpublished manuscript.

5. GFAP, Annex 7, Art. I, par. 3.

6. GFAP, Annex 6, Appendix.

7. These numbers, like most relating to displaced persons, should be treated as rough estimates. For more information on the reliability and politics of refugee statistics, see Jeff Crisp, "Who Has Counted the Refugees? UNHCR and the Politics of Numbers," Working Paper no. 12 (Geneva: Policy Research Unit, UNHCR, June 1999).

8. There was also a significant displacement of as many as 300,000 ethnic Serbs from Croatia to the FRY during the government's 1995 military offensives in Krajina. See International Crisis Group, "The Balkan Refugee Crisis: Regional and Long-term Perspectives," 2 June 1999; UNHCR, *A Regional Strategy for Sustainable Return of those Displaced by Conflict in the Former Yugoslavia,* 17 June 1998.

9. UNHCR, "Information Notes: Bosnia and Herzegovina, Croatia, the Federal Republic of Yugoslavia, the Former Yugoslav Republic of Macedonia, and Slovenia," May 1996, p. 11.

10. Ibid.; United States Committee for Refugees (USCR), "Country Report: Bosnia and Herzegovina," *World Refugee Survey 1997.*

11. Statement by Sadako Ogata, United Nations High Commissioner for Refugees, at the Peace Implementation Conference for Bosnia and Herzegovina, London, 9 December 1995. Available online at http://www.unhcr.ch/refworld/unhcr/hcshpeech/09de1995.htm.

12. UNHCR, "Returns Summary to Bosnia and Herzegovina from 01/01/96 to 31/12/99." Available at: http://www.unhcr.ba/Operations/Statistical%20package/1.htm.

13. Ibid.

14. Ibid.

15. Ibid. Although it should be noted that a small number of those Croat and Bosniac refugees repatriating to the Federation chose to return to areas where they would be among the ethnic minority. See the chapter section "Minority Returns."

16. In 1999, repatriation dropped to 31,650 from the 1998 level of 110,000.

17. CRPC and UNHCR, *Return, Local Integration, and Property Rights* (Sarajevo: UNHCR, November 1999). The ICG gives a slightly higher number of 381,000, with 223,000 Bosnian Serbs in the FRY, 30,000 Bosnian Croats in Croatia, and another 128,000 Bosnians throughout western Europe—the majority in Germany. ICG, "The Balkan Refugee Crisis: Regional and Long-term Perspectives," 2 June 1999, pp. 2–3.

18. ICG, *Minority Return or Mass Relocation?* 14 May 1998.

19. For example, a U.S. State Department program resettled 53,603 Bosnians between 1998 and 1999. USCR, "Refugees Admitted to the United States by Nationality, FY 86–99." Available online at http://www.refugees.org/world/statistics/wsr00_table7.htm.

20. Since these numbers only account for collective centers supported by international funds, this figure underestimates the dependence of IDPs on collective centers for basic shelter and sustenance. See, UNHCR, "Information Notes," 14.

21. UNHCR, "Returns Summary."

22. Ibid.

23. See discussion in Chapter 3 on "Minding the Security Gap." For more detail, see Louis Sell, "The Serb Flight from Sarajevo: Dayton's First Failure," *Eastern European Politics and Societies* 14, no. 1 (winter 2000): 179–202.

24. Author interviews, Sarajevo, November 1996.

25. In 1997, 70 percent repatriated to such areas; 90 percent did so in 1998, according to USCR, "Country Report: Bosnia and Herzegovina," *World Refugee Survey 1998;* USCR, "Country Report: Bosnia and Herzegovina," *World Refugee Survey 1999.*

26. "Slouching Towards Bosnia," *Harper's* (August 2000): 88. It has been estimated that complete mine removal in Bosnia may take as long as thirty years.

27. As Serbs battered the convoy with rocks and sticks, fifteen people were wounded, one of whom later died. USCR, "Country Report: Bosnia and Herzegovina," *World Refugee Survey 1997.*

28. USCR, "Country Report: Bosnia and Herzegovina," *World Refugee Survey 1999.*

29. USCR, "Country Report: Bosnia and Herzegovina," *World Refugee Survey 1998.*

30. Previously, Bosniacs, Croats, and Serbs all had distinctively different license plates. For more information on the OHR role, see European Stability Initiative (ESI), "Reshaping International Priorities in Bosnia and Herzegovina: Part 2, International Power," chap. 3. Available online at http://www.esiweb. org/rep3-3.html.

31. USCR, "Bosnian Minorities: Strangers in Their Own Land," *Refugee Reports,* October 1997. Available online at http://www.refugees/org/world/ articles/bosnians_rr97_10.htm.

32. UNHCR, "Open Cities Status Report," 1 August 1999. Available online at http://www.unhcr.ba/opencity/9908BH1.html.

33. Ibid.

34. Ibid.

35. See USCR, "Bosnian Minorities."

36. ESI, "Interim Evaluation of Reconstruction and Return Task Force (RRTF)," 14 September 1999. Available online at http://www.esiweb.org/ Report2-1999.html.

37. OHR, "Property Law Implementation Plan (PLIP)," unpublished paper.

38. UNHCR, "South-Eastern Europe Information Notes," 30 June 2000. Available online at http://www.unhcr.ch/world/euro/seo/infonotes/000630.pdf.

39. This commission was originally titled the Commission for Displaced Persons and Refugees. GFAP, Annex 7, Art. XII, par. 3.

40. CRPC, *Return.*

41. RRTF, "An Action Plan in Support of the Return of Refugees and Displaced Persons in Bosnia and Herzegovina," March 1998, p. 32. Available online at http://www.ohr.int/rrtf/r9803-00.htm.

42. More precisely, 25,421 cases. See USCR, "Country Report: Bosnia and Herzegovina," *World Refugee Survey 1999.*

43. These numbers are estimates. See ESI, "Interim Evaluation."

44. OHR, "Property Law Implementation Plan (PLIP)," 4.

45. See, for example, UNHCR, "Registration of Repatriates in the

Republika Srpska and Entitlement to Identity Documents, Food Assistance and Medical Care," April 1999, available online at http://www.unhcr.ba/Protection/PTB/RS99.htm; and UNHCR, "Extremely Vulnerable Individuals: The Need for Continuing International Support in Light of the Difficulties to Reintegration upon Return," November 1999, available online at http://www.unhcr.ba/Protection/PTB/EVIexec.html.

46. USCR, "Country Report: Bosnia and Herzegovina," *World Refugee Survey 1997*.

47. UNHCR, Humanitarian Issues Working Group, "Update on Durable Solutions for Refugees and Displaced Persons in the Context of the Dayton Agreement," 29 November 1999, available online at http://www.unhcr.ch/world/euro/seo/hiwg/99_5.htm; CRPC and UNHCR, *Return*.

5

Economic Reconstruction and Development

Bosnia's economy had had problems even before the dissolution of Yugoslavia. The 1980s were a period of general economic decline for the country in which the economic gap between Yugoslavia's republics widened, exacerbating tensions within and among them.[1] Compared to the other republics, Bosnia's prewar GDP per capita was higher only than that of the poorest republic, Macedonia; much lower than that of Croatia or Slovenia, the two wealthiest; and 32 percent less than the Yugoslav national average.[2] Unemployment was more than 20 percent in 1990.[3] Bosnia's economy, heavily dependent upon exports within Yugoslavia and to the Eastern bloc, was further threatened by the political and economic transitions of the Velvet Revolution. Unlike Croatia and Slovenia, for whom secession from Yugoslavia had projected economic benefits, the Bosnian economy was neither prosperous nor independent enough to provide much incentive for this course of action.

The war dealt a devastating blow to this already vulnerable economy. The conflict seriously damaged or destroyed much of Bosnia's infrastructure, industrial base, and capacity for productive economic activity. The war also took an enormous toll on "human capital": more than half the population were forcibly displaced, killed, or wounded, and tens of thousands of those Bosnians with the most mobility—largely, the professional and best-educated segments of the population—left the country more or less voluntarily. By 1995, Bosnia's per capita GDP had dropped to less than $500, or roughly 20 percent of its prewar total, and unemployment had reached 80 percent.[4] When the international community pledged at Dayton to put Bosnia back together again, it therefore took on an enormous economic task.

The Bosnian constitution agreed upon at Dayton imposed immediate practical constraints upon economic reconstruction and development. As a result of new power-sharing arrangements, the Bosnian central state, Federation, and Republika Srpska divided areas of responsibility that integrally affected economic development in the country as a whole. The central government had authority over customs, monetary policy, international financial obligations, and interentity infrastructure such as transport, communications, and energy. The entities had responsibility for tax and customs administration as well as any economic and social policies not explicitly given to the center. Notably, the entities retained all customs and tax revenue collected on their territory. The central state, meanwhile, had no independent source of revenue and had to rely entirely upon transfers from the two entities for financing.[5] Dayton called for the establishment of a Central Bank, to be led for its first six years by a non-Bosnian governor appointed by the International Monetary Fund (IMF).

Dayton made no explicit mention of international assistance in Bosnia's economic recovery. It was widely understood at the time, however, that the World Bank would take the lead in Bosnia's reconstruction, and the IMF would play a crucial role for refinancing the potentially crippling foreign debt that Bosnia had inherited upon declaring independence from the Federal Republic of Yugoslavia. The World Bank actually began planning for postwar Bosnia as early as January 1995, when it held a discreet meeting with Bosnian officials in Warsaw.[6] In October 1995, after the cease-fire but before Dayton negotiations, the World Bank also led a joint assessment mission to Bosnia with the IMF, the European Bank for Reconstruction and Development, the European Commission, and the U.S. Agency for International Development (USAID), all of which quickly become key players in Bosnia's economic recovery. The result was a plan for a three- to four-year multisector strategy to rebuild the country, termed the Priority Reconstruction and Recovery Program (PRRP), with an anticipated price tag of $5.1 billion.

Shortly after Dayton, the first of five major donor pledging conferences was held in Brussels in December 1995, where fifty countries and twenty-seven international organizations pledged a total of $615 million. Subsequent pledging conferences yielded even greater totals: April 1996 ($1.23 billion), July 1997 ($1.1 billion), May 1998 ($1.25 billion), and May 1999 ($1.05 billion).[7] In total, the international community committed nearly $5.25 billion at these five pledging conferences jointly organized by the World Bank and European Commission. As initially pledged, these resources were intended to be allocated toward physical reconstruction ($3.193 billion, or 61 percent of total), institutional development and transition ($840 million, or 16 percent of total), restarting the economy ($740 million, or 14 percent of total), and other peace implementation activities ($455 million, or 9 percent of total).[8] Despite differences over strategy and tactics, international economic actors appeared to agree on the priorities for Bosnia's postwar economy: first, facilitating the transition from a war economy to a peace economy; and second, completing the transition from a socialist economy to a market economy.

TRANSITION FROM WAR TO PEACE

As the country emerged from war, Bosnia faced the immediate task of physical reconstruction. An only slightly less immediate need was to invigorate the economy in order to create jobs and establish a base for postwar political stabilization.

Physical Reconstruction

Early donor and economic efforts focused overwhelmingly on the physical reconstruction of the country.[9] During the war more than 2,000 kilometers of main roads, seventy bridges (including all those leading to Croatia), all railway lines, and multiple airports were either made inoperable or destroyed. About half of Bosnia's electricity network was damaged. Damage to telecommunications was so extensive that telephone call completion rates dropped to barely 2 percent of those placed.[10] Many basic community resources had also become targets of ethnic cleansing. Roughly one-third of housing stock was heavily damaged, and another 5–6 percent destroyed.[11] Municipally provided services, such as water and heat, had been deliberately sabotaged, leaving many without heat and at least half of the population without regular access to water. In addition, infrastructure for social services, such as health care and education, also needed rapid resuscitation. Nearly one-third of health care facilities were destroyed by the war, and hundreds of thousands of Bosnians were left with serious physical or psychological injuries. The education system was similarly devastated by the war, with about 60 percent of all schools damaged, destroyed, or requisitioned for military use and most of the teaching staff either displaced or otherwise unable to work.[12]

On both fronts of network infrastructure and community services, international assistance made significant progress possible. According to a comprehensive May 1999 joint World Bank–European Commission report, by that time power generation had increased to about 78 percent of prewar levels, and telecommunication networks had been greatly improved, largely because of the introduction of new cellular technology.[13] At least 65 percent of formerly damaged roads had also been repaired, as had most bridges, and major railway lines had been made at least technically operable. Significant strides had also been made in repairing Bosnia's damaged housing stock, with at least 25 percent rebuilt that could shelter an estimated 400,000 people.[14] Water supply had been relatively quickly restored to prewar service levels. Most primary schools had been rebuilt, and reconstruction of secondary schools and universities had gotten under way, as had repair or new construction of hospitals, dispensaries, and clinics. Reviving municipal heating had been less successful: although the situation had largely been remedied in Sarajevo, at least thirty smaller cities and towns in Bosnia had heating systems still in need of repair. As of May 1999, Republika Srpska as a whole had yet to gain regular access to natural gas because of disputes over its outstanding prewar debt.[15]

Where such efforts have achieved only partial success, the explanation centers on the unavoidably political nature of reconstruction in the Bosnian context. Attempts to put unified networks in place for the country, for instance, ran quickly afoul of political interests to keep Bosnia divided. Although the electrical grid has been mostly repaired, for example, interentity connections have been delayed by administrative and political obstacles, not technical ones. Interentity rail traffic has also been discouragingly low, at merely 25 percent of prewar levels from 1996 through 1998, because of political resistance to implementing agreements on technical and administrative cooperation.[16] In telecommunications, even as cellular technology enabled quick resuscitation of some communication, it also quickly created cellular fiefdoms, particularly for Croatian companies operating in western Bosnia.[17] Furthermore, moderate success in physical reconstruction is matched by frustration in both the education and health sectors at a lack of interentity and intra-Federation cooperation, as Bosniacs, Croats, and Serbs continue to maintain segregated medical facilities and different curricula for schools. The medical sector also is heavily dependent upon international NGOs and expatriate professionals.

Economic Development

A second priority among international implementers was to restart economic activity, primarily through private sector initiatives. The challenge for Bosnians and implementers both was that the prewar economy had little to recommend it once Yugoslavia lost privileged access to

Eastern bloc markets with the end of the Cold War. Bosnia thus had not just to recover from war but to redesign the basis of its economy.

Prior to the war, Bosnia was heavily industrialized, with industry and mining accounting for 51 percent of its GDP in 1990.[18] Heavy industry, including military-related production, dominated in what would subsequently become Federation territory, and light manufacturing was prevalent in what would later become Republika Srpska. The timber industry was also important in Bosnia, with Bosnia's forests providing 30 percent of timber reserves in the former Yugoslavia.[19] Large-scale agriculture contributed far less to Bosnia's prewar economy, given the generally mountainous and heavily forested nature of the terrain.

Unsurprisingly, the war brought industrial production to a halt: industrial output in 1995 was estimated to have been merely 9 percent of its prewar level.[20] The war also had a seriously detrimental effect upon the timber industry and agriculture. Much of Bosnia's timber was shot through with metal fragments from combat, significantly lowering its market value. Large stretches of potentially arable land were also strewn with landmines and abandoned. By the end of the war, food production had dropped by an estimated 50 to 70 percent, and more than 80 percent of the population depended upon international food aid.[21]

In most sectors, industrial capacity had not fully recovered nearly five years after the war's end. The industries that have revived the most quickly have been those that produce primarily for the local market. Other parts of the industrial base, particularly those dependent upon imports for production, have been slower to recover, and by 1998, industrial production overall had only reached 30 percent of its prewar output.[22] Industrial revival faces additional challenges beyond the effects of war, including loss of access to previously protected markets, dramatically increased imports related to the reconstruction effort itself, and reduced tariffs demanded by international insistence upon rapid economic liberalization.[23]

The economic issue with perhaps the greatest potential political consequence is that of unemployment because stabilization of a peace may depend heavily on absorbing demobilized combatants into productive labor and seeing that a "peace dividend" reaches the broader population. Lack of economic opportunities has multiple adverse effects: on refugees and IDPs, whose judgment about return is influenced by the prospect for decent livelihood; on the newly demobilized, for whom criminal activity is a tempting option; and upon the country's segmented electorate, whose economic disadvantage provides fertile ground for nationalist explanations of their relative poverty.

Unemployment reached more than 80 percent in 1995, from a pre-war high of 30 percent in 1991.[24] In the first two years of implementation of the Dayton Accords, some strides were made on aggregate employment. However, the distribution of new jobs was dramatically skewed toward the Federation, generating powerful resentment among Serbs that international assistance was partisan. In 1997, unemployment was reduced to 50 percent in the Federation but remained as high as 90 percent in Republika Srpska because of the lack of international aid upon which most new employment depended.[25]

Increasingly, donors and implementers recognized that their with-holding of international aid to Bosnian Serbs was directly undermining the larger goal of enabling return to Serb areas and reintegration of the country. As a result, the international strategy began to shift toward seeking Serb interlocutors who might be considered more favorable toward Dayton's integrationist elements and whose participation in implementation would make it politically acceptable for international assistance to flow to Serb areas. In mid-summer 1997, Biljana Plavsic emerged as the first such candidate. Shortly thereafter, the United States and some western European governments, in close collaboration with OHR, embarked on a very explicit campaign to promote political plu-ralism in Republika Srpska. They also opened new channels for interna-tional assistance as contributions to RS radically increased from the mere 7–8 percent of total donor funds expended in Bosnia from 1995 to 1997 to a level of nearly 20 percent of funds for ongoing or completed projects in the first half of 1998.[26]

Relatively quickly, a more equitable pattern of employment genera-tion was established. By the fourth quarter of 1999, official unemploy-ment was 42 percent in the Federation and 39 percent in Republika Srpska. Official statistics also indicated that wage levels in Republika Srpska were nearly 70 percent as high as those in the Federation.[27] Although still a disparity, this nonetheless represented a vast reduction in interentity inequality compared to the immediate postwar years and, thereby, a positive development for the peace process as a whole.

TRANSITION FROM SOCIALISM TO CAPITALISM

Foreign Debt

Bosnia's transition from war to peace has been complicated by the country's simultaneous transition from a socialist to a market economy.

At the end of the war, the country immediately had to contend with the question of its foreign debt, much of which derived from Bosnia's share of the debt accumulated by the former Yugoslavia. Yugoslavia had accumulated a total external federal debt of $15.3 billion by 1991, which it had only sporadically serviced. As one of the six former republics, Bosnia was effectively in default on a $1.9 billion share of this debt (which had since increased to $3.4 billion because of interest) upon gaining independence.[28]

Creditors were fairly responsive to the situation in which Bosnia found itself, and the country was able to negotiate more favorable terms through a series of negotiations with international financial institutions (IFIs) and both state and commercial creditors. In 1995, Bosnia gained membership in the IMF and was able to use a bridging loan to clear arrears of $50 million.[29] In 1996, Bosnia reached a related agreement with the World Bank in which Bosnia's outstanding debt of $625 million was rescheduled over a thirty-year period.[30] In return for these concessions on debt servicing, Bosnia accepted such standard IFI conditions on its fiscal and monetary policy as the adoption of an IMF standby arrangement and World Bank timelines for instituting cost recovery mechanisms.[31]

Once these arrangements with international financial institutions were in place, Bosnia further negotiated a compromise with the Paris Club of creditors in October 1998 to reduce its debt by 67 percent to a total of $528 million, including $232 million in principal and $296 million in past due interest.[32] Two months later, Bosnia also reached an understanding with the London Club of commercial creditors to reduce the country's obligation by 86 percent to $394 million in total.[33] It took until August 1999, however, for Bosnia's two entities to agree on the distribution of entity transfers to the central state for debt servicing, with the Federation assuming two-thirds of the burden and RS taking the remaining one-third.[34]

Despite these comparatively favorable conditions for debt reduction, servicing foreign debt remains a significant burden on the Bosnian state budget and a drain on donor funds. Debt servicing accounted for 60 percent of the central state budget in 1998 and has been projected to require annual payments of $200–$250 million through 2005.[35] In 2002, Bosnia is scheduled to begin paying down the principal on its foreign debt, and in 2006 the principal payments on Bosnia's concessional postwar reconstruction loans will also require servicing.[36] In other words, the state's external debt payment obligations will increase substantially in the near future, just as donor assistance is likely to diminish.

Monetary and Fiscal Policy

The Dayton Agreement called for Bosnia to establish a new Central Bank that, for the first six years, would operate as a currency board.[37] As such, it would maintain monetary stability, particularly relative to foreign currencies, by using interest rates as its lever while holding money supply and exchange rates constant.

This reliance on a currency board has had mixed results.[38] On the one hand, it facilitated creation of a common currency in the country, which was important for both economic and political reasons. For several years after Dayton, three mutually exclusive currencies remained in circulation in Bosnia: the Croatian kuna was used in Croat areas, the Yugoslav dinar in Serb territory, and the Bosnian dinar or, more frequently, the German deutsche mark, in Bosniac areas. Soon after the Central Bank began operations in 1997, an interim common currency went into widespread circulation, the konvertible marka (KM).[39] The establishment and widespread distribution of a stable, common currency removed a major obstacle to economic recovery and eventual reintegration.

However, the concern about fiscal discipline that partly motivated the reliance on a currency board approach was problematic in a postwar setting with high demands on public spending. Bosnian public expenditures averaged 62 percent of GDP between 1996 and 1998, which had to be financed entirely through a combination of donor contributions and locally generated revenue since the state could not increase the money supply or issue new debt.[40] The World Bank and some donors also pushed the Bosnian government to curtail overall expenditure, including on social services, and to adopt a system of "cost recovery" that placed a particular burden on the general population to cover state recurring costs.

Privatization, Corruption, and FDI

Privatization of the Bosnian economy was also seen by IFIs, major donors, and other segments of the implementation coalition as a priority for the new state. The rationale for privatization was multiple: to help revive productivity in a manner that would be sustainable in a post–Cold War economy, reduce the government's fiscal burden, and reduce the power of state monopolies.[41] Privatization was also central to the broader objective of economic liberalization. Since Dayton, Bosnia has enacted a series of regulatory and institutional reforms in order to create a more favorable environment for private sector development and foreign direct investment (FDI). Both entities have passed legislation and set up agencies to regulate privatization, banking, capital markets, and corporate conduct. Notably, the state-level law on privatization was adopted only after OHR imposed it by decree in July 1998.

Meanwhile, the scope and implications of corruption in Bosnia have been widely debated. The issue of corruption entered public discussion prominently in 1998 as a result of a report by the EU's Customs and Fiscal Assistance Office (CAFAO) that showed widespread fraud and abuse.[42] Although some reports alleged that as much as $1 billion of international assistance may have been misappropriated during the first four years of Dayton implementation, any consideration of financial malfeasance in Bosnia should be put in perspective of postwar and postsocialist economies in general.[43] The World Bank, among other donors, has also reported that its funds have generally been used accountably. Due to the sensitivity of this issue, the OHR established an Anti-Fraud Unit after the Bonn PIC meeting of December 1997, and the Bosnian government has requested assistance from the international NGO Transparency International. The stakes in this controversy are high since allegations of corruption—let alone the fact of it—jeopardize continued donor support for peace implementation in Bosnia.

Perceptions of corruption and heightened political risk also discourage FDI. To date, international investors are neither assured that their funds will be safe nor convinced that the Bosnian economy will generate sufficient profits to offset that risk in the near to medium term. Thus, although there has been economic growth in Bosnia, it has been driven almost entirely by donor reconstruction and development projects, not a large-scale resumption of privately financed and self-sustaining economic activity. To put this in quantitative terms, the World Bank estimates that Bosnia received $130 million total in FDI for 1997 and 1998, whereas the Bosnian Ministry of Economic Relations and Foreign Trade estimated a much lower figure of only $73 million total FDI from late 1995 through the end of 1998.[44] When one compares these numbers to the level of donor assistance in the same period—approximately $2.8 billion—it becomes clear that aid, not investment, has been the engine of Bosnia's postwar economy.[45]

ASSESSMENT

International efforts to help Bosnia make a dual economic transition from war to peace and from a command to a market economy had notable achievements by 2000. Much of the country's physical infrastructure had been significantly rebuilt. Some private sector activity had emerged, and a stable common currency was in widespread circulation. An institutional framework has also begun to be put in place, including establishment of a Central Bank and the beginnings of a legal and regulatory framework that will enable the country to attract both domestic and foreign investment.

Where the economic dimension of implementation has faltered, however, has been in its unavoidable links to other, more political arenas of peacebuilding. First, political conditionality imposed on the RS at an early stage had an adverse impact on economic recovery, employment, and thus refugee returns in the entity. Implementers furiously debated the question of conditionality from the beginning. The World Bank opposed any imposition of political conditionality as a direct violation of its own charter and as detrimental to an efficient reconstruction effort. The United States, EU, and OHR argued instead, if to varying degrees, that compliance with Dayton implementation should be the condition for international assistance. For reasons ranging from insufficient compliance with demilitarization provisions to lack of cooperation with ICTY and obstruction of refugee returns, significant amounts of assistance were withheld from the Serb entity. As a result, RS received only 2 percent of bilateral international assistance during the first two years of Dayton implementation.[46] An additional rationale for directing the bulk of international assistance to the Federation was that it had suffered more war damage. Serb authorities did not help their own cause by boycotting the first donor conference in November 1997.

In practice, the international community remained divided during the implementation effort. World Bank projects largely avoided linking their assistance to compliance with Dayton or other political factors. Bilateral donors, by contrast, were mostly comfortable with political conditionality. Even if one agrees with the notion of political conditions upon aid, however, one should impose them coherently and equitably in the context of a larger strategy to consolidate peace. In the Bosnian case, it took years for donors to coordinate their efforts to impose conditions on authorities, which has only been accomplished with the ascendance of OHR as a focal point for such issues. In the interim, donors imposed their own conditions or no conditions, making their efforts less than effective. Moreover, from a Serbian perspective, it was not entirely clear why they were punished for not allowing minority returns when no Serbs were able to return to Bosnian Croat areas or even to any appreciable extent to Sarajevo.

Second, the early emphasis on rapid physical reconstruction— whether because of obvious material need or because of organizational habit among donors to focus on concrete, visible projects—required working through existing authorities. Funding that flowed to and through these politicians and bureaucrats helped further empower them, and none were particularly supportive of Dayton's integrationist goals.

Third, imposing fiscal austerity upon state budgets in an immediate postwar context, let alone proposing regressive cost-recovery policies, indirectly increases socioeconomic insecurity among the population. Even more, it fosters resentment and competition over scarce resources, making it much harder to "de-nationalize" political debate and foster political moderation. This tension between the fiscal austerity and monetary stabilization policies preferred by international financial institutions and the demands of postwar societies for quick infusions of spending has been increasingly recognized, though resolving the tension in practice remains a recurring challenge.[47]

Fourth, privatization has had a very problematic impact in Bosnia, exacerbating corruption and thereby discouraging increased FDI while not spurring enough new economic activity to compensate. This issue is hardly unique to Bosnia, which has simply repeated in a postwar Balkan context many of the same mistakes as privatization in Russia, for example. In both cases, the policies were motivated significantly by a desire to counterbalance the power elites who controlled state-owned enterprises. In Bosnia, as analogously in Russia, however, selling off public assets to private interests actually enhanced the position of these elites, many of whom were the private purchasers of formerly state-held assets. In Bosnia, this dynamic was exacerbated by the presence of a swath of war profiteers and allies of the ruling elite who had enough liquid assets to enjoy preeminent purchasing power.[48]

NOTES

1. Susan L. Woodward treats these issues centrally in her explanation of Yugoslavia's collapse. See *Balkan Tragedy: Chaos and Dissolution After the Cold War* (Washington, DC: Brookings Institution, 1995).

2. David Woodward, *The IMF, the World Bank, and Economic Policy in Bosnia* (Oxford: Oxfam, 1998), p. 11.

3. Economist Intelligence Unit, *Country Profile: Bosnia-Herzegovina 1994–1995* (London: Economist Intelligence Unit), p. 16.

4. European Commission and World Bank, *Bosnia and Herzegovina 1996–1998 Lessons and Accomplishments: Review of the Priority Reconstruction and Recovery Program and Looking Ahead Towards Sustainable Economic Development*, May 1999, pp. 15, vi. Available online at http://www.worldbank.org.ba/wbinba/blue%20book%20bosnia.pdf.

5. In a 2:1 ratio from the Federation and Republika Srpska.

6. Zlatko Hertić, Amela Šapčanin, and Susan Woodward, "Bosnia and Herzegovina," p. 319 in Shepard Forman and Stewart Patrick, eds., *Good Intentions: Pledges of Aid for Postconflict Recovery.* Center on International Cooperation Studies in Multilateralism (Boulder, CO: Lynne Rienner Publishers, 2000).

7. Hertić, Šapčanin, and Woodward, "Bosnia and Herzegovina," 325–326; Office of the High Representative, *Economic Reform and Reconstruction in Bosnia and Herzegovina* 2, no. 5 (June 1999), available online at www.ohr.int/newsletter/eco-0205.htm.

8. European Commission and World Bank, *Bosnia and Herzegovina 1996–1998,* 1; Office of the High Representative, *Economic Reform and Reconstruction in Bosnia and Herzegovina.*

9. For example, the two largest sectors in terms of firm donor commitments from 1996 to 1997 were "energy" ($456 million) and "housing" ($451 million). Hertić, Šapčanin, and Woodward, "Bosnia and Herzegovina," 325, table 8.1.

10. European Commission and World Bank, *Bosnia and Herzegovina 1996–1998,* 3–5.

11. Ibid., 7. In the Federation, 33 percent of housing stock was damaged and 6 percent destroyed; in Republika Srpska, 29 percent was damaged and 5 percent destroyed.

12. Ibid., 11–12.

13. Ibid., 4.

14. Ibid., 6.

15. Ibid., 8.

16. Economist Intelligence Unit, *Country Profile: Bosnia and Herzegovina 1999–2000,* 15, 34.

17. Confidential interviews, UNMIBH, Sarajevo and Banja Luka, November 1996.

18. Economist Intelligence Unit, *Country Profile: Bosnia and Herzegovina 1999–2000,* 17.

19. Ibid., 24.

20. Ibid., 25.

21. European Commission and World Bank, *Bosnia and Herzegovina 1996–1998,* 16.

22. Economist Intelligence Unit, *Country Profile: Bosnia and Herzegovina 1999–2000,* 25.

23. Ibid.

24. European Commission and World Bank, *Bosnia and Herzegovina 1996–1998,* 15. Even official unemployment statistics must be qualified since they exclude those employed in gray market or black market activities as well as those who have not yet been registered as unemployed.

25. Susan L. Woodward, "Bosnia After Dayton: Transforming a Compromise into a State," pp. 151–152 in Robert Rothstein, ed., *After the Peace: Resistance and Reconciliation* (Boulder, CO: Lynne Rienner Publishers, 1999).

26. Hertić, Šapčanin, and Woodward, "Bosnia and Herzegovina," 348. RS received only DM 113 million out of the DM 1.5 billion spent in Bosnia in

1995–1997. Some months after the regime change in November 1997, aid began to flow to western RS but continued to be withheld from eastern RS because of allegations that people in that area were harboring war criminals. RS then received DM 400 million out of the DM 2.1 billion expended in the first six months of 1998.

27. See Office of the High Representative, *Economic Reform and Reconstruction in Bosnia and Herzegovina* 3, no. 4 (May 2000). Available online at www.ohr.int/newsletter/eco-0304.htm.

28. Woodward, *The IMF,* 18.

29. Ibid., 20.

30. Ibid.

31. The standby arrangement was implemented under normal rather than concessional credit terms, whereas the cost-recovery mechanisms entailed cutting back humanitarian assistance donations. Both of these policies were hotly debated and contested by the Bosnian government. See Hertić, Šapčanin, and Woodward, "Bosnia and Herzegovina," 350.

32. Ibid., 29.

33. Ibid.

34. Economist Intelligence Unit, *Country Report: Bosnia and Herzegovina 4th Quarter 1999,* 25.

35. Economist Intelligence Unit, *Country Profile: Bosnia and Herzegovina 1999–2000,* 29–30.

36. Economist Intelligence Unit, *Country Report: Bosnia and Herzegovina 4th Quarter 1999,* 25; Benn Steil and Susan L. Woodward, "A European New Deal for the Balkans, *Foreign Affairs* (November–December 1999): 96.

37. GFAP, Annex 4, Art. VII.

38. For a general critique of the use of currency boards in postwar contexts, see Woodward, *The IMF,* 32–34.

39. Economist Intelligence Unit, *Country Profile: Bosnia and Herzegovina 1999–2000,* 26.

40. European Commission and World Bank, *Bosnia and Herzegovina 1996–1998,* 33.

41. Ibid., 35. Although many state-owned enterprises due for privatization are in the industrial sector and probably would be better off under eventual private management, this influential report also mentions such essential public services as electric power and distribution, heat and natural gas, water, and roads as potential candidates for one-time revenue generation by the state.

42. See, for example, Hertić, Šapčanin, and Woodward, "Bosnia and Herzegovina," 365, note 73.

43. Chris Hedges, "Leaders in Bosnia Are Said to Steal Up to $1 Billion," *New York Times,* 17 August 1999. Hertič, Šapčanin, and Woodward, "Bosnia and Herzegovina," 350–353.

44. Economist Intelligence Unit, *Country Report: Bosnia and Herzegovina 3rd Quarter 1999,* 27.

45. Hertić, Šapčanin, and Woodward, "Bosnia and Herzegovina," 330–332.

46. Ibid., 348.

47. For an early analysis of such issues in the context of El Salvador, see

Alvaro de Soto and Graçiana del Castillo, "Obstacles to Peacebuilding," *Foreign Policy* 94 (spring 1994): 69–83; see Office of the High Representative, *Economic Reform and Reconstruction in Bosnia and Herzegovina* 4, no. 1 (October 2000). Available online at http://www.ohr.int/newsletter/eco-0401.htm.

48. General Accounting Office (GAO), *Bosnia Peace Operation: Crime and Corruption Threaten Successful Implementation of the Dayton Peace Agreement*, GAO/NSIAD-00-156, July 2000, available online at http://www.gao.gov/archive/2000/ns00156.pdf; Economist Intelligence Unit, *Country Profile: Bosnia and Herzegovina 1999–2000*, 20.

6

Reunification

At the end of the war, Bosnia was de facto divided among three authorities: the Bosnian Serbs, led by the SDS of Radovan Karadzic; the Bosniacs, led by the SDA of Alija Izetbegovic; and the Bosnian Croats, led by the HDZ, with a clutch of leaders tightly tied to Croatian president Franjo Tudjman. Each party was backed by its respective armed forces, the VRS, the ABiH, and the HVO. Bosnian Serbs very clearly controlled territory under their authority, the new entity of Republika Srpska. Between Bosniacs and Bosnian Croats, there was greater ambiguity: even though the two had been ostensibly at peace since 1994, much of central Bosnia was a patchwork of towns and villages held respectively by one or the other—sometimes, divided between them—and larger portions of the country's southwest were clearly under the singular authority of the Croats.

The premise underlying the Dayton Agreement was that accommodation could be made between this effective separation (and those who sought to deepen it) and the professed aspiration among Bosniacs and much of the international community for a unified state. Since the war had significantly advanced the country's segregation, the principal challenge in implementation was to rebalance the equation in favor of unity. Philosophically, most of the governments who had committed themselves to supporting Dayton implementation also opposed ethnic exclusivity, which further strengthened the significance they attached to reunification.

Dayton's primary mechanisms for reunifying the country were institutional and demographic. First, the agreement defined the architecture of a new Bosnian state. A new constitution incorporated into the Dayton text detailed how power was to be shared among Bosnia's three parties and two entities within a single state via the composition of executive and legislative bodies at all levels of government. These institutions were to begin functioning with the first round of postwar elections. Although the Dayton constitution did not fully address the constitutional balance between Bosniacs and Croats within the Federation, it was assumed that the Federation constitution authored in 1994 would govern their relations.[1]

Second, this political craftsmanship was meant to be bolstered from below by Dayton's provisions to reverse ethnic cleansing. A steady flow of returning refugees was supposed to be well under way by the time of the first elections, which, ostensibly, would give an advantage to nonnationalist parties and thereby increase momentum toward reunification.[2]

Initially, international implementers tended to accompany their approaches—top-down or bottom-up—with frequent appeals to the principle of "multiethnicity" and the international commitment to it. As the first year of implementation wore on, it became increasingly clear that this tack—whose advocates became known among critics as "multi-multis"—provoked resentment more than effect and that ordinary Bosnians were most interested in a restoration of normality, whether this implied the remixing of populations or not.[3] By the second year after Dayton, implementers toned down the rhetoric, though they ramped up practical efforts to encourage minority returns, as has already been discussed. They also began to focus anew on aspects of reunification that bore more on the day-to-day practicalities of interaction across borders than on reinforcing the principle of multiethnicity per se.

UNIFICATION FROM ABOVE

Beyond the efforts to rejoin military and police forces already discussed, Dayton called for the Bosnian parties to commit to share power in a postwar state by participating in joint political institutions. At the state level, Bosnia has a presidency composed of three individuals, a Bosniac and Croat elected by voters in the Federation and a Serb elected by voters in the RS; and a bicameral parliament composed of a House of Representatives (forty-two members, of which two-thirds are elected by Federation voters and one-third by RS voters) and a House of Peoples (fifteen members, of which two-thirds are appointed by a Federation legislature and one-third by the RS legislature). Bosnia's ministers are appointed by the president, subject to approval by the parliament, and cannot exceed a Federation to RS ratio of 2:1. Each minister has two deputies from each of the other ethnic groups, and the chairmanship of the Council of Ministers rotates weekly among them. Significantly, the Bosnian state was given no independent judicial branch, though the Dayton Agreement does provide for a constitutional court.

At the entity level, the RS has no explicit obligation to share power, whereas the Federation is like a mini-Bosnia, explicitly constituted in order to balance the interests and offices of the Bosnian Croats and Bosniacs whom it governed. The RS has a president and National Assembly (it has 140 members and is the body charged with nominating the five RS members of the Bosnian House of Peoples), both directly elected by voters registered in the RS.

In the Federation, the president is not directly elected but rather appointed and approved by the Federation's two legislative bodies—the Federation House of Representatives and Federation House of Peoples—only the former of which is directly elected by voters registered in the Federation. The president and the vice president, who are assumed to be split between Bosniacs and Croats given their method of selection, rotate roles on an annual basis. The Federation's elected House of Representatives has 140 members; the House of Peoples, which is appointed by canton governments, has sixty members, split evenly between Bosniacs and Croats.

Below the entity level, ten cantons exist within the Federation, whose assemblies are directly elected by Federation voters and are charged with appointing executive governors and ministries. Both the Federation and RS also contain municipalities, whose assemblies are directly elected by voters in each entity, respectively, which bodies in turn appoint municipal mayors.

The institutionally weakest level of government is the single state at the top. Dependent on budgetary transfers from the entities, with neither an army, police force, nor judiciary of its own, it has relatively little leverage over lower levels of government. At the entity level, the Federation is also comparatively weak vis-à-vis its ten cantons. Cantons enjoy the power to tax and exclusive authority over police, internal security, and judicial matters. In several areas, cantons share with the Federation a coequal authority that they are only enjoined to divide "as appropriate" after consultation, including authority over immigration and asylum, implementation of legislation related to citizenship, social welfare, and communications and transport policy.[4]

Broadly, implementers have tried two approaches to get joint institutions up and running. First, they established additional forums for consultation and monitoring of compliance. On the military side, Dayton established a Joint Military Commission under the chairmanship of the IFOR/SFOR commander to hear complaints of noncompliance and determine an appropriate international response. On the civilian side, Dayton called for the establishment of a Joint Civilian Commission and any necessary subcommissions to be chaired by the High Representative or his designate, also to hear complaints of noncompliance and determine the necessary response.

Within the Federation, a Federation Forum was set up alongside a previously appointed Federation mediator. The forum is chaired by OHR and is composed of OHR's Principal Deputy High Representative, the president and vice president of the Federation, and two international officers who are agreed upon by the other three. Frustrated progress within the Federation led to the later creation of a Federation Implementation Council (on 14 March 1996) to hear complaints of noncompliance and within six weeks issue a final and binding decision, which could include removal of any offenders from office.

A second approach was to impose conditionality on various forms of international assistance. From the beginning, statements from the OHR described the linkage between compliance with Dayton and the flow of international assistance. Early efforts at conditionality were significantly weakened, however, by the absence of a uniform international approach that effectively rendered talk of conditionality meaningless.

Getting Bosnia's joint institutions to function even minimally has been an ordeal, however. The sheer complexity of the institutional arrangements and constant rotation of roles has made it easy for parties to obstruct the functioning of various offices. Every issue from the timing of meetings to their location, let alone their agenda, has become an occasion for resistance. Meetings have been boycotted, as in 1996, when the newly elected Serb member of the Bosnian presidency, Momcilo Krajisnik, was absent at his own inauguration ceremony in Sarajevo, or when HDZ members walked out of the inaugural session of the Sarajevo canton assembly.[5] Delay has been the norm on fronts ranging from nominations to high office (it took three months to nominate two co-chairs of the Council of Ministers),[6] rules of procedure (six months after the 1996 elections, the Federation House of Representatives had yet to adopt these), and international credit for reconstruction (which was held up for months in 1996–1997 because the three presidency members could not agree who should sign international aid contracts). Even when legislation has been developed, it has frequently been ignored or has remained ineffectual in the absence of further implementing legislation. Such frustrations were especially common in the early period of implementation, as might be expected, but they have not disappeared: in 2000, a new dispute among the Council of Ministers rendered the body "dysfunctional" for months, according to the PIC.[7]

UNIFICATION FROM BELOW

As frustration with the pace of reunification grew in 1997, international implementers also began to recognize that greater attention had to be paid to reforms that would effectively empower individual Bosnians to begin reintegrating the country from below, which represents the third main approach to integration. A major element of a ground-up approach, though to date one of its least effective ones, has been the series of strategies developed to enable "minority" return, which has already been discussed.[8] More intriguing were some of those items that became known as "Sintra" issues because they were first raised prominently at a PIC meeting in Sintra, Portugal, in May 1997.

At Sintra, the PIC leveled its strongest criticism yet of the separatist dynamics that continued to prevail in Bosnia—"the international community will not tolerate any attempts at partition, *de facto* or *de jure,* by anyone"—and the meeting issued a series of directives to Bosnian leaders, complete with deadlines and threat of sanction, to make headway on multiple issues.[9] Some of these were symbolic—for example, the design of a common flag, composition of a common anthem, and appointment of international ambassadors. However, more of them were extremely concrete and potentially powerful: agreement on common currency, common citizenship laws and passports, a joint telephone system, and uniform car registration, as well as amendment of discriminatory property laws and remedy of funding shortfalls for the CRPC and Commission on Human Rights.

The significance of such issues should not be underestimated because each was linked to the instruments by which nationalist parties maintained control over areas under their authority. By the end of the war, each party had effectively created its own exclusion zone, with its own symbols and media of exchange. A small but hardly unique example is the central Bosnian town of Gornji Vakuf. The war left Gornji Vakuf physically and institutionally divided between Bosniacs and Bosnian Croats, much like Mostar. As a result, on alternate sides of the narrow street that had been its former frontline, residents used two different currencies (the Croatian kuna versus the Bosnian dinar), two different international telephone codes (the Croatian 385 versus the

Bosnian 387), two different automobile license plates (the Croatian checkerboard emblem versus the Bosnian coat of arms), two "different" languages, and two different names for the town (the Bosniac Gornji Vakuf versus the Croatian Uskople).

The obstacles to social and economic interaction posed by such divisions were severe, let alone to the "freedom of movement" called for under Dayton. Vehicle licenses, in particular, were a problem, since any car could immediately be identified as Bosniac, Croat, or Serb and therefore become a target of violence. UNHCR's bus service for would-be returnees was one way to avoid this hazard. An obvious longer-term solution was a system of licensing that was ethnically neutral.

It seemed clear to many observers that most Bosnians wanted to see such barriers removed. In December 1997, the Open Broadcast Network hosted a call-in television show to gauge the level of support for common license plates and a common Bosnian passport, one of the other practical items on the international agenda. In forty-eight hours, 19,500 people called in their views, with 19,000 registering support for unmarked licenses and a single passport. Only 500 were opposed.[10] Indeed, when neutral license plates went into wide circulation in May 1998, the effect on freedom of movement was "titanic." Within several months after their introduction into use, close to 1 million plates were in circulation, representing approximately 85 percent of the driving public.[11] At major interentity crossing points monitored by the UN specifically for the purpose of evaluating the impact of the licenses, cross-entity traffic increased by 300 percent once the plates were in circulation.[12]

It is important to note that there are more complex sources of resistance to unification efforts than simple intransigence among elites. To return to the example of Gornji Vakuf, its divisions left the town not only with rival license plates, currencies, and phone codes but also with two sets of public institutions, such as health clinics and schools. Both Bosniac and Croat communities would have benefited from unifying the schools, allowing the two districts to consolidate scarce equipment along with their two artificially small student bodies that forced the schools to operate on reduced schedules.[13] When the schools were divided, however, both had also hired more teachers, even if at reduced salaries. An obvious and immediate implication of reunification, therefore, was that half the teachers were likely to lose their jobs, which created an additional source of resistance to rejoining the schools in the absence of other job prospects.[14] Such dynamics indicate how critical it is for international implementers to understand well the practical linkage between reunification and other arenas of implementation, especially at the local level. Yet even though many engaged in peace implementation on the ground fully recognized such interdependence, developing mechanisms by which their respective organizations can work jointly to address such issues has been a chronic weakness in Dayton implementation.

ASSESSMENT

Rejoining Bosnia from either the top or the bottom has been an arduous and only partly successful effort. Formally, joint political institutions eventually began to function as originally planned, despite early resistance among Bosnian leaders. More concrete accomplishments have been made on the practical level: a common currency (the konvertible marka pegged to the deutsche mark) went into circulation in mid-1998, as did the uniform license plates.

If one looks below form to substance, however, progress on reunifying institutions and practical aspects of daily life has been less impressive. The power-sharing institutions envisioned at Dayton operate in buildings flying a common flag, but they rarely make decisions of significance. Progress on the Sintra issues also occurred comparatively late in the game to affect freedom of movement at the critical early stage. Moreover, achievements on both fronts have increasingly resulted only by being imposed through the authority of the High Representative and other key implementers. The PIC expressed anxiety over this pattern early, noting "with concern" in mid-1998 that "almost all progress has required the continued and intensive efforts from the international community."[15] Items ranging from the common flag and anthem to common currency, passports, and citizenship have all required international imposition in the manifest absence of a willingness to move these forward among Bosnians, at least with the timeliness insisted upon by implementers. As late as 2000, this pattern showed no sign of diminishing: inaction on the joint State Border Service prompted OHR to impose this law in January 2000,[16] and Bosnia's new draft election law was only rendered operative for the fall 2000 elections by OHR action.[17] To date, the most salient feature of peace implementation in Bosnia has been the emergence of what has been variously called a "trusteeship in all but name" and a "creeping protectorate," with troubling implications for the sustainability of any unity accomplished.

NOTES

1. Dayton included a short side agreement on Federation implementation but largely avoided confronting the possibility that the Federation might not exactly cohere. See *Dayton Agreement on Implementing the Federation of Bosnia and Herzegovina,* 10 November 1995, and *Bosnia and Herzegovina: Constitution of the Federation,* 18 March 1994.

2. The agreement stated: "By election day, the return of refugees should already be underway, thus allowing many to participate in person." It also allowed that a citizen "may, however, apply to the Commission to cast his or her ballot elsewhere." GFAP, Annex 3, Art. IV.

3. Confidential interview, OHR, Sarajevo, November 1996.

4. Constitution of the Federation, III. Division of Responsibilities Between the Federation Government and the Cantons, Art. 2, points (d), (e), (f), and (g).

5. For some time, the HDZ continued to resist cooperation with parliamentary and presidential bodies, demanding a renegotiation of power-sharing arrangements with the SDA that would give them a legal status within Bosnia closer to that of the RS.

6. On 12 December 1996, these were named as Haris Silajdzic and Boro Bosic.

7. See discussion online at http://www.ohr.int/docu/p20000505a.htm.

8. As of early 2000, significantly higher levels of minority return appeared to have been occurring. According to ICG's analysis, the increase in returns stems from refugee impatience, increased international effectiveness, and a notable shift in majority and minority group psychology. See ICG, "Bosnia's Refugee Logjam Breaks: Is the International Community Ready?" 30 May 2000.

9. "Political Declaration from Ministerial Meeting of the Steering Board of the Peace Implementation Council," 30 May 1997, par. 18, available online at http://www.ohr.int/docu/d970530a.htm.

10. Interview with Jacques Paul Klein, 5 March 1998.

11. Interview with David Harland, 6 March 1998.

12. Seeing this initiative through took considerable ingenuity and diligence from UN Civil Affairs, where the original idea was hatched, and from OHR, which helped pull off the feat. At each stage, the UN had to anticipate ways that the plates might be secretly coded, defeating the purpose. They developed a system in which licenses used numbers and only those letters common to Cyrillic and Latin alphabets (A, E, J, K, M, and T). Actual license numbers were generated in one location, shuffled before being produced in another, and taken to yet a third that coordinated their distribution. When authorities wanted to charge drivers DM 50 for a license to deter their use—they cost DM 9 to produce—international officials brokered a compromise that enabled the price to be set far lower. To encourage their rapid use by motorists, neighboring governments—for example, Austria and Hungary—rallied to insist that their borders could only be crossed by Bosnian drivers using the new plates.

13. Gornji Vakuf had approximately 1,200 students and Uskople 700. Interview with Sanja Krnjajic, Youth Center, Gornji Vakuf, 9 March 1998.

14. Interviews with Sanja Krnjajic (Gornji Vakuf) and Phillip Pierce (Travnik) (9 March 1998).

15. "Declaration of the Ministerial Meeting of the Steering Board of the Peace Implementation Council," Luxembourg, 9 June 1998, par. 5, available online at http://www.ohr.int/docu/d980609a.htm.

16. OHR Press Release, State Border Service Law, 13 January 2000.

17. Despite pleas and pressure from the international community, the Bosnian parliament had not ratified the law by May, prompting OHR to enact it de facto by incorporating it into the existing PEC rules and regulations. The text of the law is available online at http://www.ohr.int/docu/p20000505a.htm.

7

Democratization

Postwar Bosnia faced daunting challenges for a newly democratic state. Its three leading parties were monoethnic; more habitually authoritarian than democratic; and, predictably, even more so as a result of their experience during the war, when political and economic power was heavily concentrated among a small politico-military elite. The prospect of conducting national elections within six to nine months as stipulated under the Dayton Accords was also slim in a damaged country with more than half of its voting population either displaced within the country or living as refugees in nearly a dozen host countries. More sobering than the logistical challenge this situation posed was the implication that, in a new "democratic" era, the effect of the war's ethnic cleansing had been a brutal gerrymandering of Bosnia's electorate. Furthermore, the country faced a new need to protect human rights, both to account for their past abuse and to prevent their future violation. Indeed, after the war, what could be called Bosnia's "democratic deficit" had reached a new depth.

The international community had three broad objectives for the democratization of postwar Bosnia. First, national elections had to be held in order to establish the power-sharing institutions that would form the bedrock of postwar political accommodation. These took on an added importance in the absence of any provision for interim international or indigenous administration, since some form of governing authority was needed in order to proceed with other dimensions of international assistance and Bosnian reconstruction.

Second, implementation presented an opportunity to restart the process of Bosnian democratization that had been interrupted by war. Although Bosnia, like the rest of former Yugoslavia, was atypical among communist societies, democratizing its political institutions and culture still implied a serious transition even without the impact of civil war. Bosnia's first round of free elections in 1990 had produced victory for the leading nationalist party, the SDA, and put the question of electoral reform high on the agenda, with the SDA advocating a majoritarian system and "minority" parties strenuously rejecting it in favor of variations on the existing power-sharing theme. Nor had the country begun to weaken the hold of its weighty state sector or the grip of party elites upon its extensive bureaucracy, which had, if anything, been strengthened by the war rather than weakened.

Third, and not least from the perspective of international implementers, a successful round of national elections was seen as the ticket to international exit from the country, which had been vociferously promised, especially to the U.S. Congress and public. For all three objectives, the question was not just whether each might be accomplished but whether achievement of one—notably, holding early national elections—would jeopardize success in the others.

ELECTIONS

National elections were to be held within six to nine months of the accord's signing, or by September 1996, and the Dayton Agreement provided for municipal and cantonal elections but did not insist that they be held as well.[1] A national ballot would take place only if conditions pertained in the country that ensured a comparatively free and fair election, specifically freedoms of expression, press, association, and movement; the right to vote without fear or intimidation; and, importantly, "a politically neutral environment."[2]

The OSCE was to supervise all aspects of elections, including verification of acceptable conditions. Its Head of Mission would chair a Provisional Election Commission composed of both international and Bosnian members who would establish all electoral rules and regulations until Bosnia could set up its own permanent commission. Each of the three parties was represented on the PEC, though its international chair was authorized to designate additional members as he or she saw fit, and his or her decisions were final and binding.[3] PEC rulings overrode preexisting national laws, and the body was authorized to take unspecified remedial action should any person or party violate electoral rules.[4] Through the PEC, the OSCE had to determine rules governing eligibility and registration of parties and candidates, eligibility and registration of voters, method of voting, codes of campaign conduct, and the role of domestic and international observers.[5]

The PEC could also establish subsidiary bodies as it deemed necessary, and in the years since Dayton it has created a potent network of election-related offices.[6] These include a judicial Election Appeals Sub-Commission (EASC), which is charged with enforcing compliance with the PEC's rules and regulations;[7] a National Election Results Implementation Commission (NERIC), established by the PIC to monitor implementation of election results, especially at the municipal level;[8] and a Media Experts Commission, supplanted in 1998 by an Independent Media Commission (IMC), which is the primary regulatory body for electronic media in Bosnia.[9]

The 1996 Elections

Dayton put the first round of elections on an exceptionally tight and chaotic schedule. In early 1996, it had still not been decided whether the national ballot would be preceded by local elections or precisely when these would take place in the months between June and September.[10] Furious debate arose over the wisdom of holding them on schedule and the readiness of the OSCE to preside over them.[11] There were technical concerns (voter registration for refugees did not begin until June, and a full set of rules governing electoral conduct was published only in July), but of far greater worry was the political sway of nationalist leaders—especially Radovan Karadzic and other high-level indictees—and the manifest absence of the "politically neutral" conditions called for by Dayton.

The OSCE, under Swiss foreign minister Flavio Cotti as its chairman-in-office and headed in Bosnia by U.S. diplomat Robert Frowick, was under enormous pressure to go through with elections on time. Many U.S. and European diplomats—including High Representative Carl Bildt—expressed the view that elections were the essential first step in getting Bosnia's new joint institutions off the ground, which themselves were crucial to knitting the country's fractured communities back together. This view was reinforced by a tendency, especially among Western policymakers, to equate democracy with elections and neglect the broader dimensions of democratization. In the absence of a mandate for the international exercise of transitional authority, there was also a need simply to put Bosnian interlocutors in place to begin the process of postwar reconstruction.[12] Even more decisive was the imperative of holding elections before IFOR's mandate came to an end. Importantly, 1996 was also a presidential election year in the United States, and the Clinton administration had publicly promised that U.S. troops would be out of Bosnia by December.

Cotti resisted allowing the elections to go ahead for some time. Like other critics, he predicted, accurately as it turned out, that the national elections would restore to power the wartime leaderships least likely to commit themselves to building peace, only this time with democratic legitimacy.[13] When Cotti finally assented to elections in mid-June, he publicly expressed his reluctance, arguing that it was "imperative" that the months between June and September be devoted to creating the conditions that still did not exist: "If no actions are undertaken right now against the indicted war criminals, it can be taken for granted that the elections will very quickly give way to developments diametrically opposed to those which they are expected to yield."[14]

In the event, the elections were held in September on schedule. Technically, the elections had problems, though the extent and impact of these has been debated. The International Crisis Group, one of the tougher critics of the 1996 elections, identified the following problems: a higher number of voters (almost 2.2 million officially registered and counted) than was technically possible, poor handling of refugee registration and out-of-country voting (not terribly surprising, since registration for more than 800,000 refugees began just three months before the elections), a shortfall of between 5 percent and 15 percent of registered voters from official lists, the decision to locate several polling stations at sites of major wartime violence, technical decisions made without full disclosure to candidates and voters, ballots that were not in the custody of accountable parties when they were moved from polling stations to counting centers, and the mystifying OSCE decision to destroy all ballots one week after votes were certified based on a regulation adopted the day before elections were held.[15]

An ostensibly "technical" question that turned out to have enormous strategic impact was the question of voter registration. According to Dayton, voters in both national and local elections were expected to vote in the municipality where they were registered by the last prewar census in 1991. Given the dispersion of Bosnia's population, especially the large numbers who were internally displaced, Dayton also provided that a citizen "may, however, apply to the Commission to cast his or her ballot elsewhere."[16] Remarkably enough, the agreement nonetheless stated this expectation: "By Election Day, the return of refugees should already be underway, thus allowing many to participate in person."

Because it quickly became clear that the return of refugees and internationally displaced persons would not be significantly under way in time, a mechanism had to be found to make good on Dayton's promise that people could apply to vote elsewhere while not also opening the door to massive electoral fraud. The PEC thus developed a form—the now notorious "P-2" form—that allowed those displaced externally or internally to register "in the municipality in which they intend to live in future." The only curb on abuse of this allowance was that P-2 voters had to cast their ballot in person and not as an absentee; but effectively the P-2 provision created a legitimate mechanism and an open invitation for electoral fraud on a large scale. After the 1996 national ballot, the P-2 was acknowledged as having been a significant mistake in implementing Dayton's electoral provisions. Indeed, one of the main reasons for continual postponement of municipal elections was the need to develop an alternative means of enabling voting among the displaced, since any P-2-like mechanism in the small voting pools of Bosnian municipalities would have been destructively consequential.[17]

Of even greater concern was the prevailing environment of generalized insecurity and partisanship in the period before elections, especially in the absence of any confidence that NATO or the United States would stay a course longer than December 1996. As Cotti and others had noted, indicted war criminals still dominated political life,[18] opposition politician figures had been targets of attack,[19] freedom of media and of movement was minimal, civilians who belonged to minority communities were subject to systematic violence and intimidation by authorities, and brute uncertainty prevailed among Bosnia's residents and its refugees about whether their country could be rebuilt as one or would be split into three. In short, Bosnia's climate was one of such manifest insecurity that the rational vote for people to cast was for the nationalist parties, which most reliably, if narrowly, had always promised to protect their interests.[20]

The results of the September 1996 elections surprised no one. The three leading nationalist parties were victorious in all offices. For the Bosnian presidency, 60 percent of the Bosniac vote went to the SDA's Izetbegovic, 67 percent of the Bosnian Croat vote to the HDZ, and 67 percent of the Bosnian Serb vote to the SDS. For the RS presidency, 59 percent of the vote went to the SDS. For the Bosnian House of Representatives, Federation voters put SDA and HDZ members in 24 out of 28 seats, and RS voters elected 9 out of 14 seats for the SDS. In the Federation House of Representatives, 114 out of 140 seats went to a combination of the SDA and SDS, and in the RS National Assembly, 45 of 83 seats went to the SDS. Interestingly, nationalist parties fared comparatively better in the Federation than in the RS.

Later Electoral Rounds (1997, 1998, and 2000)

Between the 1996 ballot and 2000, Bosnia conducted four more statewide rounds of polling for various levels of government: two rounds of elections for state and entity offices in September 1998 and

November 2000; two sets of municipal elections, the first in September 1997 after three postponements, and the second in April 2000. In addition, a special entitywide election to the RS National Assembly was held in November 1997, after the split in Serb leadership prompted Biljana Plavsic to defect from the SDS.

At each stage, the OSCE made technical improvements—for example, in 1997 votes in the RS were counted at the polling station instead of being moved to other locations first.[21] The PEC and its subsidiary bodies also actively used their regulatory and sanctioning powers to support nonnationalist parties and to marginalize what are seen as extremist parties. Parties judged in violation of PEC rules and regulations have been prohibited from fielding candidates, and individual candidates have been stricken from party lists; parties already on ballots have been decertified; and "pecuniary or other appropriate penalties" have also been imposed.[22] Increasingly, these OSCE-led bodies have also aimed to leverage their authority through coordination with OHR and even SFOR. The main achievements have been to get governing structures up and running and, gradually, to support more moderate opposition parties, which had their best showing in the municipal ballot of April 2000.

Still, winning seats is a very different thing from actually occupying them. In the 1997 municipal election, parties representing Bosnia's displaced made striking gains, but new officials were no more able to return to villages run by an opposite nationality than were their constituents. In Srebrenica, for instance, Bosniac candidates won 52 percent of the municipal seats but were unable to assume them for months.[23] The OSCE refrained from certifying municipal election results until the resultant governing authorities actually functioned, and for many municipalities, it had to appoint "special envoys" to push the cause of election implementation. In some cases, notably Srebrenica, SFOR had to provide area security simply for local councilors to go to work.[24] In a sense, one should not be surprised at the resistance. Any achievements made by nonnationalist parties will by definition come at the expense of the status quo parties, independent of how authentic their nationalist spirit.

A particular challenge faced by implementers was that the constitutional framework established at Dayton inhibited the formation of nonnationalist constituencies and the electoral success of nonnationalist parties. Undoubtedly, this result was not intended but posed no less serious of a constraint for being inadvertent. Under Dayton, a series of offices can only be elected by residents of one entity or the other, removing any incentive for contenders to these positions to build a political base that crosses ethnic lines. Proposals have been floated for how to overcome this obstacle, but reform is delicate, since it is likely to entail amending the constitution, which some argue implies amending the Dayton Agreement itself.

The approach thus far has instead been incrementalist, seeking through PEC rulings a kind of "soft" constitutional amendment. The Draft Election Law tabled in October 1999 made significant improvements on the existing system. These included the use of open party lists, the assignment of some parliamentary offices to fixed constituencies, a preferential ranking system of election of the Bosnian presidency, a ban on candidates who occupy property belonging to refugees or displaced persons, and tight regulation of campaign expenditures. Ratification of the law requires passage by Bosnia's two parliamentary bodies as well as implementing legislation by entity parliaments. In the absence of full ratification, the draft law has been incorporated into the PEC's Rules and Regulations.[25]

BEYOND ELECTIONS

Elections are only one element of democratization, of course. Over the long term, successful democratization in Bosnia, as elsewhere, will involve a dense network of political, institutional, and even cultural changes, including reform of civil-military relations, development of a legal environment that fosters accountability, political party and civil society development, and growth of independent media. In the short term, however, the democratic process in Bosnia was particularly challenged by the perceived and actual impunity of persons indicted for war crimes, the practical frailty of the human rights institutions established under Dayton, and a highly politicized media environment. Obstacles in each of these areas rendered elusive the "neutral political environment" called for under Dayton as an essential condition for elections and democratic development.

Accountability for War Crimes

A central question immediately upon the war's end was whether and how quickly persons indicted for war crimes would be apprehended for trial or otherwise removed from the political scene. Dayton obligated Bosnian authorities to comply with all international human rights and enforcement efforts, expressly including the ICTY at The Hague.[26] Dayton also authorized the NATO-led force to apprehend any indictees.

ICTY was the first international war crimes tribunal established since Nuremberg and Tokyo and was authorized by the UN Security Council to prosecute "persons responsible for serious violations of international humanitarian law committed in the territory of the former Yugoslavia since 1991."[27] Even though ICTY could issue indictments, conduct prosecutions, render judgments, and impose sentences, it was entirely dependent on others to bring indictees into custody unless they voluntarily surrendered, as some have. The primary burden was upon governments in whose territory indictees resided or traveled: Bosnia, Serbia, and Croatia. In the absence of their robust cooperation with international criminal proceedings, however, ICTY depended on international enforcers to bring suspects into their custody.

In the first year and a half of Dayton implementation, PIFWCs enjoyed near total impunity. Few surrendered to The Hague voluntarily, both Bosnian entities and neighboring governments gave them safe haven, and IFOR essentially abdicated its authorized responsibility to apprehend indictees with whom it was in effective contact. As a result, indictees traveled widely and freely throughout Bosnia, indeed even through NATO checkpoints, without fear of being arrested. Meanwhile, those Bosnian wartime leaders who had been indicted, from Karadzic on down to mid-level leaders, exercised either overt or covert influence over Bosnian politics.

Over time, NATO forces in Bosnia showed greater willingness to apprehend indictees, but a few crucially important fugitives remained—notably Radovan Karadzic and Ratko Mladic, who were indicted for genocide and crimes against humanity among other human rights and humanitarian violations.[28] By September 2000, from a total of sixty-seven outstanding public indictments, international forces (primarily SFOR) detained twenty indictees, twelve alleged war criminals voluntarily surrendered, and nine others were arrested by national police (outside Bosnia). Twenty-six remained at large.[29]

To the extent that international criminal proceedings have a broader objective of cultivating respect for the rule of law, the ICTY experience has an additional limitation that, for all its judicial independence, its activities cannot avoid being implicated in the politics of implementation. At an early stage, ICTY was faulted by some critics—and the bulk of the Serbian population—for pursuing indictments and prosecutions disproportionately against Serbs, particularly vis-à-vis their treatment of Croatians and Bosnian Croats. In public forums, ICTY responded to this criticism particularly by showing greater commitment to investigations of Croatian offenses during the offensives of 1995 as well as a willingness to investigate alleged NATO transgressions during the air war over Kosovo.[30] Such demonstrations of a balanced approach occurred late in the implementation process, however, after perceptions of ICTY prejudice had deepened into conviction. Legal status as an ICTY indictee also relates closely to international interventions in Bosnian politics, including the dismissal of officials.[31]

Human Rights

The Dayton Agreement was also meant to ensure that sustainable mechanisms to address violations of human and civil rights were put into place in Bosnia. Dayton called for the establishment of a Commission on Human Rights, consisting of a Human Rights Chamber and a Human Rights Ombudsman.[32] In addition, the Federation has its own Human Rights Ombudsman. Dayton's human rights annex also included an unprecedented array of provisions in which the authorities agreed to be party to sixteen international and regional human rights conventions, which would ostensibly give Bosnians greater legal protection than any other citizenry in the world.[33] In a significant derogation of sovereignty, the Bosnian constitution also gave primacy to the European Convention for the Protection of Human Rights and Fundamental Freedoms (and its protocols) over domestic legal provisions.

From the perspective of implementation, the human rights provisions were less robust. No one implementer had the lead. Both the OSCE and the Council of Europe had authorized roles, as did the European Court of Human Rights. International jurists sat on the constitutional court and in the Human Rights Chamber; the Human Rights Ombudsman was an international civilian appointed by and reporting to the OSCE. The UN High Commissioner for Human Rights (UNHCHR) had a Special Rapporteur in the region (Elisabeth Rehn, who subsequently served as head of UNMIBH). The UN, because of its work with the police, added a Human Rights Office for the IPTF, a tough role since Bosnia's police were often the perpetrators of human rights abuses. Simply because of their mandated activities, UNHCR, UNMIBH, and European Community military monitors could not avoid observance or knowledge of human rights abuses. Meanwhile, OHR tried to coordinate the whole, first through raising to the level of Deputy High Representative its chief human rights adviser and, later, through creation of a Human Rights Coordination Center (HRCC).

Perhaps unsurprisingly, Dayton's human rights provisions generally lacked sufficient commitment by or coordination among international actors.[34] Beyond the sheer complexity of the system, which Manfred Nowak describes as "so sophisticated that it can never of course be implemented," Dayton's human rights provisions are essentially toothless.[35] The constitution does not specify enforcement mechanisms for human rights and leaves this responsibility to the entities rather than the state. In the absence of commitment from entity leaderships to enforce full human rights protection—unlikely, given that police are estimated to be the main violators—enforcement would either have to be international or nonexistent.[36] However, NATO-led forces have assiduously avoided this potential role, and IPTF has been generally ill-equipped for it.

Meanwhile, international financing of Bosnia's human rights institutions has been dramatically short of what would be needed to raise their profile and effectiveness, both at the state and Federation level. For example, as of October 1998, the Human Rights Ombudsman's office had opened over 50,000 provisional files and registered over 2,500 cases requiring a decision but had only adopted fifty-seven final reports and referred eighty cases to the Human Rights Chamber.[37] Interestingly, the vast majority of cases brought to the Ombudsman were complaints about property—either alleged illegal usurpation of it or damage done to it.

The Bosnian judicial system more broadly remains compromised by the following factors: overt political influence—particularly on matters of refugee and IDP return; insufficient funding that compels judges to ask local authorities or private sources for operating costs; political interference with appointments and dismissals; a lack of security for judicial personnel; shortages of judges in some areas; a lack of equipment and legal resources; separate Bosniac and Croat courts in Canton Six and Canton Seven; and serious caseload backlogs in a number of courts.[38] At the end of 1998, the UN launched an ambitious effort to assess the Bosnian judicial system in order to develop a serious program for judicial assistance. In a telling comment on implementation, the UN effort was conducted parallel to work on related issues at the OSCE, and the resources needed for the UN initiative (several additional legal experts) were fiercely opposed by the United States on the UN Security Council. Only after extensive lobbying by other governments was the effort allowed to proceed.

Independent Media

From early in the course of the war, the baleful influence of the former Yugoslavia's state media was widely recognized. Though Yugoslavia also had a critical mass of professional and independent-minded journalists, the media market in the country was dominated by subsidized state media, especially in radio and television. These were used to promote the parties' respective war efforts and, more to the point, their respective hold on political power. In the words of a particularly acerbic businessman in Banja Luka, the most accurate way to describe the relationship between conflict and the Bosnian media was that "war is television news by other means."[39]

The international community's approach to supporting media independence in Bosnia has changed over time, from ambitious but disappointing initial efforts, such as the first year of the Open Broadcast Network, to lower-key but more effective efforts, such as Swiss support for independent Radio FERN.[40] Generally missing among early efforts was a coherent strategy that would harness the respective projects of various agencies to longer-term support for independent media. International implementers have also been criticized for their only modest engagement with local media in Bosnian languages and for undermining their own longer-term goal by absorbing talented aspiring journalists into international organizations—which inevitably pay higher wages than even internationally supported local media.

Despite early missteps, the international community did indeed appear to have a strategy, which is to use its own powers under Dayton—and Bonn—to put in place a regulatory framework within which independent media can flourish. This has, at times, involved expansive, sometimes dramatic restriction of media seen as nondemocratic, as when SFOR seized Serb transmitters broadcasting inflammatory content in 1997. More subtly, a regulatory framework has emerged from the decisions and rules of the IMC, which was set up in 1998 as a subsidiary body of the PEC.

The concept underlying the IMC emerged after prolonged international frustration over the pace of media reform and existing international efforts to foster it more than two years after Dayton. At the Bonn PIC meeting in December 1997, a redesign of the international approach to media was proposed that had three primary elements: monitoring, licensing authority with judicial powers, and enforcement. Within six months, the IMC was established by High Representative Carlos Westendorp to operate as "the supreme regulatory authority of electronic media" in the country.[41] Like the PEC, the IMC has been designed to become fully Bosnian over time, though only "upon a decision of the High Representative determining whether the conditions for the transfer are given."[42]

ASSESSMENT

If one evaluates international efforts according to their basic objectives, the record of implementation of Dayton's democratization agenda has been very mixed. On the positive side, Bosnia has conducted several rounds of elections with a modest degree of freeness and fairness, and as noted, nonnationalist parties have made steady if still small inroads. Though many observers have criticized the OSCE, which, unlike the UN, had never conducted elections before, its operational shortcomings should be put in context. Even a vaunted UN success like the conduct of elections in Namibia had serious flaws, taking considerable time and with an extremely high observer-to-voter ratio (by some estimates as high as 1:5). In fact, the OSCE also hired many seasoned UN electoral hands, and those elements of the Bosnian context that challenged the OSCE would likely have stymied the UN as well.[43] To put its progress further in perspective, some observers with experience have stated that Bosnia compares favorably to other postcommunist states, including Russia and Ukraine, where the level of mafia involvement in politics in both countries is much higher.[44]

A regulatory framework for electoral conduct has also been established, which provides a solid legal foundation for Bosnia's continuing political evolution. The long-term objective is for the PEC to become fully indigenous, which is more likely with the broadening of the PEC's political base in 1998 to include moderates. Not only are the enlarged PEC's judgments more likely to be fair, but also this larger body gives individuals (even from nationalist parties) the political space to support positions independent of their party's line, since such decisions can more easily be attributed to other members.[45] Eventually, the OSCE should be able to fade into simply a supportive role.

A wider spectrum of activities surrounding human rights, rule of law, media independence, and civil society development also bolsters the prospects for deepening democracy in Bosnia. On the negative side, however, the electoral system remains extremely complex, even with simplifications that have been made over time. More than seventy parties and nearly 600 candidates were represented in the 1998 elections, and voter education is much less effective than it could be.[46] Bosnia's experience has not been unlike that in other postcommunist democracies: elections swollen by large numbers of parties representing very small constituencies, parties that go their own way or join unwieldy and shifting coalitions, and complex balloting and party list systems with mathematical formulae for allocating seats. Such systems tend to favor new parties but also tend to engender fragmented, divisive electioneering and the perception among bewildered voters that the new system is unresponsive to their interests. Indeed, the Bosnian opposition is not necessarily that much of an improvement on the status quo parties, organized as it is around small, overly personalist parties and unaccustomed to a system in which accountability to one's democratic constituents has something to do with longevity in power.[47]

Strategically, international implementers have handled poorly the question of managing Bosnia's least democratic individuals and parties. At an early stage, the active influence of PIFWCs throughout the country exerted a powerful influence on popular perceptions of Bosnia's political future and on basic security. Even though apprehension of indictees has increased over time, the prolonged initial period of international inaction on this front had an immeasurably destructive impact.[48]

The favored approach has been alternately to back individual favorites or use Dayton-authorized institutions to sanction or remove certain politicians. Thus, the High Representative has increasingly acted under his "Bonn powers" to remove officials from office at all levels of Bosnian government when they have been seen to be violating the spirit of Dayton. Multiple mayors have stepped down as a result of OHR rulings. Much more dramatically, High Representative Carlos Westendorp called in March 1999 for the removal of the legitimately elected president of Republika Srpska, Nikola Poplasen. Poplasen's offense was his refusal to accept as prime minister the more moderate Milorad Dodik, who had majority support from the RS National Assembly and was favored by the West.[49]

Although this tack may accomplish the short-term objective of removing certain individuals from power, it has periodically done so at the cost of due process and popular confidence in the fairness of the system. In 1996, for instance, an EASC ruling barring the hard-line Serb SDS party from participation in elections was overruled by PEC chair Robert Barry after the SDS threatened a boycott, even though the juridical terms of reference for the EASC explicitly state that it is fully autonomous and that its decisions are final and binding.[50] Poplasen, of course, was even democratically elected—if by a slim majority of 44 to 39 percent. That the occasion of his removal was his refusal to accept as prime minister an obvious Western favorite only heightened skepticism about the move among many observers. At the very least, this approach encourages the view among many Bosnians that politicians, in the end, are less accountable to voters than to whomever wields greater power, which in the present case is the international community.

To attempt to implement democratic reforms through what are

viewed as nondemocratic methods is inherently contradictory. Ironically, this approach is also dubiously effective. Even though many mayors and others have been removed from office, preventing them from exercising effective power behind the scenes is much more difficult. In 1998, Nikola Poplasen may have been nominally de-elected, but he left neither the building nor the scene for some time.

More strategically problematic has been the relationship between electoral efforts and other aspects of Dayton implementation. No credible observer disputes that the first round of national elections, held under the conditions that then existed, solidified the position of nationalists on all sides. For students and practitioners of peace implementation, the question is whether there were viable alternatives to holding those elections on time. The reasons for the pressured calendar were multiple, though domestic political pressures within key governments supporting the implementation effort would seem to be preeminent among them. Of course, postponement of elections alone would be meaningless unless this were done as part of a broader effort to endow Dayton implementation with genuine strategic coherence among key governments and among implementing agencies.

NOTES

1. National elections entailed developing ballots for executive and legislative offices at state and entity levels: the three-person presidency of Bosnia; the president of the Republika Srpska; and the respective legislatures of Bosnia, Republika Srpska, and the Federation.

2. Annex 3, Art. I, par. 1. Portions of the 1990 Conference on Security and Cooperation in Europe "Copenhagen Document" are reproduced at the end of the Annex, further specifying aspects of democratic conduct by the parties. See also "Document of the Second Meeting of the Conference on the Human Dimension of the Conference on Security and Cooperation in Europe," Copenhagen, 1990.

3. The PEC, with seven members at the beginning, has expanded over time, first to ten and then in 1998 to a total of sixteen. The last enlargement was explicitly designed to include more moderate Bosnian voices.

4. Annex 3, Art. III, par. 2(d). Confidential interview, OSCE, Sarajevo, August 1998.

5. Subsequently established PEC Rules and Regulations allowed for party lists and independent candidates to be on ballots.

6. Its mandate is described in Annex 3, Art. III, pars. 2b–c.

7. Established in May 1996, the EASC comprises four judges (one international and one member from each of the Bosnian state, Federation, and Republika Srpska), all appointed by the OSCE Head of Mission. It rules by consensus, though the chair can decide in the event of a split, and all decisions

are "final, binding and not subject to appeal." For more, see information online at http://www.oscebih.org/easc/eng/easc.htm.

8. NERIC was established in December 1996.

9. Established in June 1998, the IMC inherited the functions of the Media Experts Commission (MEC) and expanded them. In contrast to the MEC, the IMC falls under the rubric of the High Representative's office.

10. In fact, the actual timeline for the elections was not finalized until late June 1996. See OHR, *Bulletin*, no. 8, released 23 June 1996. Available online at http://www.ohr.int/bulletins/b960623.htm#1.

11. For a representative sample of arguments in this debate, see Misha Glenny, "Decision Time in Bosnia," *New York Times,* 8 September 1996; Stephen S. Rosenfeld, "Sticking to the Dayton Accords," *Washington Post,* 23 June 1996; and Morton I. Abramowitz, "Bosnia: The Farce of Premature Elections," *Washington Post,* 24 May 1996.

12. Arguably, implementers have acquired the equivalent of such a mandate over time, between the judicial mechanisms of the OSCE and the Bonn powers of the OHR, but it did not exist in late 1996. Confidential interviews, OHR, Sarajevo, March and August 1998.

13. According to some accounts, Frowick also wanted to see tougher criteria imposed on holding elections. In a statement that is representative of the public debate, Glenny writes: "Editorial writers have joined forces with such influential commentators as the financier and philanthropist George Soros and former Prime Minister Haris Silajdzic of Bosnia. All say roughly the same thing: that holding the elections will guarantee that Humpty remains dismembered and that the results of ethnic cleansing will be sanctioned by what is a bogus democratic gesture" (Glenny, "Decision Time in Bosnia").

14. Chris Hedges, "Despite Doubts, Official Gives Go-Ahead to Bosnian Vote," *New York Times,* 26 June 1996.

15. ICG, *Elections in Bosnia and Herzegovina,* ICG Bosnia Report no. 16 (22 September 1996), available online at http://www.crisisweb.org/projects/showreport.cfm?reportid=148.

16. Annex 3, Art. IV. All Bosnian citizens over eighteen who were listed in the 1991 census were eligible to vote.

17. Confidential interview, OHR, August 1998. Another unfortunate consequence of the early problems with the P-2 form, ironically, is that Bosnian parties have seized on the issue as electoral fodder in subsequent elections, even though the form is no longer used. See OSCE press release, "Discussion of So-called 'P-2' Form Is a Travesty," 20 June 2000, available online at http://www.oscebih.org/pressreleases/june2000/20-6-p2.htm.

18. U.S. special envoy Richard Holbrooke brokered a deal on 18 July 1996, in which Radovan Karadzic agreed to step down as president of Republika Srpska and refrain from public political activities. He nonetheless remained an active figure behind the scenes.

19. The most widely reported incident was the physical attack on Haris Silajdzic, Bosnia's wartime foreign minister (later prime minister). As a candidate for a new multinational party, he was attacked on 15 June 1996 by a gang carrying SDA flags in Cazin. Jovan Kovacic, "Assault on Bosnian Leader Highlights Tension," Reuters World Serve, 16 June 1996, available in LEXIS, News Library, Reuwld File.

20. Analysts with OHR and UNMIBH note that there appeared to be a potent mixture of genuine mononationalist sentiment and fear-based allegiance. Confidential interviews, Sarajevo, August 1998.

21. Confidential interview, NGO, August 1998.

22. In an impressive gesture toward due process and transparency, all judgments of the EASC and IMC have been posted on the Internet at http://www.oscebih.org/easc/eng/easc.htm and http://www.imcbih.org.

23. ICG, "ICG Analysis of Municipal Election Results," 14 October 1997, available online at www.crisisweb.org.

24. R. Jeffrey Smith, "Local Government Hits Snag in Bosnia: Refusal to Share Power with Minorities Leads to Boycotts, Violence," *Washington Post Foreign Service,* 29 January 1998: A24.

25. For a concise critique of the draft law, which argues for it to go further, see Balkan Action Council, "Improving the Electoral Law for Bosnia-Herzegovina," 22 December 1999.

26. GFAP, Annex 6, Article XIII (4). See also, GFAP, Annex 1, Article X. Mentioned in both the military and human rights annexes of Dayton, this stipulation has been widely interpreted as obligating IFOR and its successor SFOR to apprehend ICTY war criminal indictees—a task that SFOR has only reluctantly and belatedly assumed.

27. UN Security Council, Resolution 808, 22 February 1993.

28. They were indicted by the ICTY on 25 July 1995 (case no. IT-95-5-I) and then again on 16 November 1995 (case no. IT-95-18-I). See information online at http://www.un.org/icty/glance/karadzic.htm.

29. See http://www.un.org/icty/glance/keyfig-e.htm.

30. See 1999 ICTY press releases: one example is available online at http://www.un.org/icty/pressreal/p420-e.htm.

31. See, for example, David Chandler, *Bosnia: Faking Democracy After Dayton* (London: Pluto Press, 1999), pp. 99–104. The ICTY's greatest achievement has not actually been within a Bosnian context. Rather, like the International Criminal Tribunal for Rwanda (ICTR), it has served as a needed precursor to the establishment of the International Criminal Court (ICC). Ironically, because they have inadvertently highlighted the limits of ad hoc tribunals (e.g., political manipulation and lack of resources), the ICTY and the ICTR have made a strong case for the necessity of a permanent, impartial, appropriately staffed, and fully resourced International Criminal Court.

32. GFAP, Annex 6, Art. II–XII.

33. GFAP, Annex 4 and Annex 6 (Appendix). The human rights agreements are listed as follows in the Appendix to Annex 6 of the GFAP: (1) 1948 Convention on the Prevention and Punishment of the Crime of Genocide; (2) 1949 Geneva Conventions I–IV on the Protection of the Victims of War, and the 1977 Geneva Protocols I–II; (3) 1950 European Convention for the Protection of Human Rights and Fundamental Freedoms and Protocols; (4) 1951 Convention Relating to the Status of Refugees and the 1966 Protocol; (5) 1957 Convention on the Nationality of Married Women; (6) 1961 Convention on the Reduction of Statelessness; (7) 1965 International Convention on the Elimination of All Forms of Racial Discrimination; (8) 1966 International Covenant on Civil and Political Rights and the 1966 and 1989 Optional Protocols; (9) 1966 International Covenant on Economic, Social, and Cultural

Rights; (10) 1979 Convention on the Elimination of All Forms of Discrimination Against Women; (11) 1984 Convention Against Torture and Other Cruel, Inhuman, or Degrading Treatment or Punishment; (12) 1987 European Convention on the Prevention of Torture and Inhuman or Degrading Treatment or Punishment; (13) 1989 Convention on the Rights of the Child; (14) 1990 Convention on the Protection of the Rights of All Migrant Workers and Members of Their Families; (15) 1992 European Charter for Regional and Minority Languages; and (16) 1994 Framework Convention for the Protection of National Minorities.

34. The HRCC consists of OHR, OSCE, UNHCHR, UNMIBH, and UNHCR. Critics assert that it still does not have adequate authority for coordination. See, for example, Michael O'Flaherty, "International Human Rights Operations in Bosnia and Herzegovina," chap. 4 in Michael O'Flaherty and Gregory Gisvold, eds., *Post War Protection of Human Rights in Bosnia and Herzegovina* (Boston: M. Nijhoff Publishers, 1998).

35. Manfred Nowak concludes: "A less ambitious and costly system would definitely have better served the aim of protecting human rights and developing a culture based on the rule of law." Nowak, "Lessons for the International Human Rights Regime from the Yugoslav Experience," *Collected Courses of the Academy of European Law,* vol. 8, book 2 (The Hague: Kluwer Law International, 2000).

36. Nowak, "Shortcomings of Effective Enforcement of Human Rights in Bosnia and Herzegovina," in Michael O'Flaherty and Gregory Gisvold, eds., *Post War Protection of Human Rights in Bosnia and Herzegovina* (Boston: M. Nijhoff Publishers, 1998).

37. Figures cited in Nowak, "Lessons."

38. Although a relative lack of institutional capacity is an obstacle faced by even the best judicial systems, consistent patterns of bribery and improper exertion of political influence will ultimately undermine the rule of law and impair the democratization process. For the judicial assessment, see, OHR, *HRCC Human Rights Semi-Annual Report,* April–September 1999. Available online at: http://www.ohr.int/hr-report/sr9902.htm. For further information, see a series of ICG reports, such as the most recent, "Denied Justice: Individuals Lost in a Legal Maze," 23 February 2000, available online at www.crisisweb.org.

39. Confidential interview, NGO, Sarajevo, November 1996.

40. ICG, "Media in Bosnia and Herzegovina: How International Support Can Be More Effective," 18 March 1997, available online at www. crisisweb.org.

41. See the IMC website at http://www.imcbih.org. Under the overall leadership of an internationally appointed director-general—currently, Swedish jurist Krister Thelin—the IMC is governed by a seven-member council (three international, two Bosniac, one Serb, and one Croat) whose decisions are taken by majority vote (the international chair can cast a tie-breaking vote). Its Enforcement Panel has similar membership (three international, two Bosniac, one Serb, one Croat) and decisionmaking powers. Members of both bodies have been appointed by the High Representative; in the future, they will be appointed by the European Commission, with the High Representative's consent.

42. See the IMC website at http://www.imcbih.org.

43. Ibid. It was widely acknowledged that the OSCE was given responsibility for elections because the UN was seen as discredited by Dayton's U.S. mediators and, according to some, by the Bosnian population as well. Confidential interview, OHR, Sarajevo, August 1998.

44. Confidential interview, NGO, Sarajevo, August 1998.

45. Confidential interview, OSCE, Sarajevo, August 1998.

46. Confidential interview, OSCE, Sarajevo, August 1998.

47. Confidential interviews, OHR, August 1998.

48. Recall that Momcilo Krajisnik, apprehended in June 2000, was elected as the Serb representative on the Bosnian presidency in the 1996 elections.

49. OHR press release, "Removal from Office of Nikola Poplasen," 5 March 1999, available online at http://www.ohr.int/press/p990305b.htm.

50. Confidential interview, NGO, August 1998.

8

International Authority

To date, the most striking feature of peace implementation in Bosnia has been the increasing reliance upon exercise of international authority to respond to noncompliance by the parties to Dayton, especially on issues related to unification. In the process, Bosnia has seen the emergence of a "trusteeship" model of peace implementation, which some have labeled a "creeping protectorate." The principal strategy under this model, as Susan Woodward describes it, is to override Bosnian sovereignty in the short term in order to establish a preferred foundation for building it in the long term.[1] The principal, though not exclusive, vehicle of international authority has been the Office of the High Representative, under the guidance of the Peace Implementation Council. Whether this approach has been or is likely to be effective depends not just on the single issues resolved by international decision. Any evaluation of its effectiveness must also account for the impact of such an approach on other goals of implementation, including the sustainability or democratic legitimacy of any unity accomplished. One must also differentiate between the exercise of international authority broadly and the effect of gaining trusteeship-type powers by degree and over time rather than having them from the outset.

AN EVOLVING ROLE

The trend toward trusteeship was driven largely by international frustration with the slow pace of implementation on the political side. Bosnian authorities dragged their feet as well as actively obstructed various implementation efforts, especially where power sharing, unification of institutions, and remixing of populations—that is, minority return—

have been concerned. As we argue in this volume, there was also implementer culpability for lack of progress—particularly the failure to integrate the military and civilian sides of implementation forcefully at an early stage.

Thus, at the end of 1996, although IFOR had overseen the successful implementation of Dayton's military provisions, implementers were faced with a situation in which nationalist parties had consolidated their control politically and demographically. No persons indicted for war crimes had been brought to the ICTY through any efforts of NATO; indeed, some of the more notable indictees were frequently seen in full public view enjoying a "freedom of movement" denied to much of the Bosnian population. Minority returns were negligible, and the ethnic terrain of Bosnia had actually been further cleansed in the early days of implementation, if by less malignant means than during the war. By mid-December, as a result, there was no serious consideration that IFOR would actually leave as originally planned, and its successor force, SFOR, was fairly expeditiously authorized. For these and other reasons, Dayton implementation came under heavy criticism, most of it leveled against the civilian contribution to the process.

By early 1997, implementers and the PIC began to reconsider their approach, which coincided with a changed political landscape among the PIC's major players. U.S. president Bill Clinton had been reelected and had named Madeleine Albright—whose "take no prisoners" approach to the Balkan conflict was widely known—as his new secretary of state. Tony Blair was elected UK prime minister, naming Robin Cook as foreign minister, both of whom were also considered hawkish on matters relating to the former Yugoslavia. Finally, Wesley Clark had become the new supreme allied commander in Europe, replacing the more intervention-shy George Joulwan. With this changing of the guard among major states and institutions, the opportunity was ripe for an assertive reengagement in Bosnian implementation.

When the PIC met in June 1997 in Sintra, Portugal, its central aim was to reinvigorate the implementation effort. The Sintra meeting called frank attention to noncompliance by Bosnian authorities and imposed strict deadlines for their adherence to multiple provisions. Sintra also prefigured the "Bonn powers" that would subsequently be given to the Office of the High Representative in late 1997; according to a new High Representative, Carlos Westendorp, these powers included authority over provocative media ("to curtail or suspend any media network or programme whose output is in persistent and blatant contravention of either the spirit or the letter of the Peace Agreement")[2] and potential enforcement power with respect to implementation of municipal election results.[3]

As months passed after Sintra with frail achievement in the areas identified, international frustration grew that much more, culminating in the authority granted to the High Representative by the PIC at Bonn, Germany, subsequently called the "Bonn powers." Textually, the High Representative had always enjoyed final authority over interpretation of Dayton's civilian provisions. Yet PIC governments had never before indicated their willingness to see him or her exercise it robustly.[4] By the time of Bonn, this reticence had changed. Drawing from this Dayton-given authority, the High Representative was now enjoined "to facilitate the resolution of difficulties by making binding decisions, as he judges necessary;" to take "interim measures when parties are unable to reach agreement, which will remain in force until the Presidency of the Council of Ministers has adopted a decision consistent with the Peace Agreement on the issue concerned"; and to undertake any

> other measures to ensure implementation of the Peace Agreement throughout Bosnia and Herzegovina and its Entities as well as smooth running of the common institutions. Such measures may include actions against persons holding public office or officials who are absent from meetings without good cause or who are found by the High Representative to be in violation of legal commitments made under the Peace Agreement or the terms for its implementation.[5]

In short, OHR was given both *creative authority* to develop and enact laws otherwise blocked by the Bosnian leadership and *enforcement powers* to take action against any public party, including members of the media, who were not abiding by the terms of Dayton implementation. The interpretation of Dayton rests singularly with OHR.

Since Bonn, the Office of the High Representative has resorted to using Bonn powers with regularity. Most integrationist legislation has been enacted by OHR, including laws on common currency and coinage, a common flag, a common anthem, citizenship, a uniform vehicle license, the state border service, and elections. OHR has also issued directives when it deemed appropriate, such as on the suspension of municipal authorities' legal right to reallocate socially owned property, which was being used to keep ethnic minorities from returning to their homes.

OHR has also not shied from its enforcement powers, often exercised in close cooperation with the OSCE and sometimes SFOR. Many officials have been dismissed, including those who had been elected, from individual legislators to the president of Republika Srpska.[6]

This exercise of international authority has not been limited to OHR, although the High Representative's role is particularly visible. From the beginning, Dayton conceived of a high level of long-term international involvement in Bosnia. Some implementing actors, notably NATO, were reluctant or unable to exercise the full license granted them by the peace agreement. Others, such as the OSCE, were less so. Not only did the OSCE mission in Bosnia try to use what powers it had been given through the Provisional Election Commission, it arguably exercised powers it was never even given, such as when the PEC overruled an EASC decision immediately prior to the 1996 elections. The roles played by OHR and the OSCE, particularly when combined with the wide range of international involvement in other arenas of the Bosnian polity and economy, make for a heavy "footprint" indeed of international engagement in the country.

Such extensive international involvement in Bosnian political life is unlikely to abate in the near term. For example, after expressing strong concern that Bosnian authorities had not yet decisively improved the country's investment climate by cracking down on corruption or deregulating the economy, the PIC Steering Board in April 2000 reaffirmed OHR's role in the economy, stating that the High Representative "should use his full powers to remove obstacles that choke economic growth and deprive the citizens of jobs and a fruitful economic life."[7] In Lisbon the following month, the Steering Board lamented the lack of progress in judicial and legal reform and anticipated "a continuing international presence that can oversee the work of domestic judicial selection institutions and otherwise assist in the implementation of programs." A few months later, the Steering Board agreed that OHR should establish an independent judicial commission to supervise the reform process in both entities and cantons.

ASSESSMENT

The emergence of a trusteeship model of implementation raises several issues, the very first of which is at the crux of the challenge of peace implementation. Third parties presumably only lend themselves to such efforts when belligerents are seen as unable to implement a settlement on their own. There are many reasons for this. The parties may need a third force to establish a buffer and build confidence during a fragile early peace, which is the classic peacekeeping model. The parties may also need institutional or technical assistance that is simply unavailable indigenously within a short time frame for everything from de-mining to running a postwar election. In Bosnia, a third factor was at work: the parties were far from committed to the agreement they signed, and there was likely to be heavy continuing negotiation, even enforcement, needed to ensure that they stuck to the terms of the accord. In this sense, Bosnia is one of the toughest of "tough cases" among post–civil war environments, replete with parties who were likely to act as "spoilers" and need to be managed as such by international implementers.[8] The challenge for interested governments and implementing organizations, if they recognize a tough case at the outset, is to structure their involvement in such a way that they will be well-equipped to overcome anticipated noncompliance and resistance.

The dilemma for those involved in Bosnia was posed by extra-Bosnian factors that rendered it impossible to launch from the beginning the kind of implementation operation that most observers knew would be required. The United States, as the prime mover at Dayton and the country whose military commitment to an implementation force was essential to its credibility, faced domestic political constraints that foreclosed the possibility of a peace operation with unitary civil-military command. Political positioning among other governments and organizations also led to an initial model of decentralized civilian implementation, which was manifestly the weakest foundation possible in a context that would require tough, continuing negotiation with the parties from a position of strength.

Over time, Dayton's implementers have essentially attempted to create the model with which they should have begun: tight coordination among civilian efforts with a panoply of carrots and sticks at their disposal, the capacity to override noncompliance and establish certain ground rules for a continuing peace and political process, and an integrated civil-military command. Curiously, what Bosnia's peacebuilders have tried to establish incrementally is something like the peace operation set up in Eastern Slavonia at the same time. The United Nations Transitional Administration for Eastern Slavonia, Western Sirmium, and Baranja (UNTAES) was authorized to implement the Basic Agreement between Croatia and Serbia in which Eastern Slavonia would gradually be transferred from Serb possession to Croat control. UNTAES was blessed by everything that Bosnia was not: a clear final status agreement between the key countries, with full backing by relevant international parties; a fully integrated military-civilian structure under the command of a civilian Transitional Administrator who was, helpfully, a high-ranking military officer; a dramatically ample set of military assets at the operation's disposal; a field of operation uncluttered by large numbers of other agencies; and an extremely talented head of mission and staff.[9]

Adopting such a model over time, however, has had a very different effect in Bosnia than the results that might be expected if it had been used from the outset. First, one simply loses time in which progress is not made for want of a more robust implementation effort. More troubling are the signals sent to Bosnian parties and the population at large about democratic process and legitimacy. The message of the trusteeship approach as resorted to in Bosnia is the following: if due process does not yield results, override it, at least if one has the political backing to do so. What this means is that the trusteeship method being deployed to accomplish one set of implementation objectives risks undermining others, principally those of fostering institutions and a culture of democratic accountability.

The trusteeship model has at least two other weaknesses as practiced in Bosnia. Especially because it has developed over a protracted period and only grown more intensive, there is less pressure upon Bosnian parties to resolve their disputes and figure out a way to run their country. Instead of using international authority early and in an interim fashion to establish a framework that could then be handed over to Bosnian authorities, it has been used to compensate for inaction or intransigence among Bosnian leaders, with the result that international implementers appear increasingly and intimately enmeshed in domestic Bosnian politics. The second, related weakness is that of exit. In present circumstances, the international community is in Bosnia for a very long haul.

NOTES

1. See Susan L. Woodward, "Compromised Sovereignty to Create Sovereignty: Is Dayton a Futile Exercise or an Emerging Model?" unpublished paper (Washington, DC: Brookings Institution). This section of this chapter uses the term *trusteeship* broadly as the best descriptor of the role of international implementers while recognizing that trusteeships have a more precise legal and historical meaning.

2. Ministerial Meeting of the Steering Board of the PIC, 30 May 1997, "Political Declaration," par. 70, available online at http://www.ohr.int/docu/d970530a.htm.

3. "Political Declaration," par. 64.

4. Contrast the language with that from a 1996 meeting of the PIC in Paris, when the High Representative's authority was wanly described as follows: "The High Representative may give his interpretation and make his recommendations known public [sic]."

5. Peace Implementation Conference, "Conclusions," 10 December 1997, Bonn; Section XI, pars. 2, 2(b), and 2(c).

6. For example, when a member of the RS parliament issued a thinly veiled threat against internationals prior to the NATO air war over Kosovo, he was promptly "barred indefinitely from holding further official positions in BiH." "International Bosnia Aid Sacks Serb Official over Kosovo," Agence France Presse, 8 October 1998. The official, Dragan Cavic, had "warned" that NATO action "could influence the implementation of the Dayton peace agreement" since "an attack in Yugoslavia is an attack on all Serbs living on the territory of former Yugoslavia."

7. Communiqué by the Steering Board of the Peace Implementation Council, Sarajevo, 4 April 2000, available online at http://www.ohr.int/docu/p20000404a.htm.

8. Stephen Stedman, "Implementation Strategies," in Stedman, Donald Rothchild, and Elizabeth M. Cousens, eds., "Strategies, Organizations, and Consequences: Explaining the Outcome of Peace Implementation in Civil Wars." Vol. 2 of "Ending Civil Wars," a joint research project of the Center for International Security and Cooperation and the International Peace Academy. Unpublished manuscript.

9. Interestingly, the UN Transitional Administrator, U.S. general Jacques-Paul Klein, was dispatched at the end of his Eastern Slavonia assignment directly to Bosnia, first to act as Principal Deputy High Representative at OHR under Carlos Westendorp and subsequently to run UNMIBH as its Special Representative of the Secretary-General.

9

Evaluating the Dayton Project

Having examined Dayton implementation in five key arenas of international activity—security, displaced persons, the economy, reunification, and democratization—this volume now turns to an evaluation of the Bosnian operation as a whole. To do so seriously requires clarifying certain basic methodological questions, such as how to determine the objectives of implementation, and, in turn, what criteria should be used to evaluate its accomplishments. For better or for worse, the Bosnian experience has almost from the beginning been accompanied by a vocal body of "evaluators" in the media and the advocacy and policy communities. These have frequently conflated and confused the terms of debate, mixing up short-term and long-term goals, assuming rather than arguing the importance of single-issue objectives to the broader peace, and failing to distinguish between broad objectives for Bosnia and the arguably narrower range of goals that can be met by international third parties.

OBJECTIVES AND CRITERIA

One approach to determining the objectives of Dayton implementation (and hence appropriate criteria for evaluation) is to assess progress directly against the goals laid out in the GFAP. This approach, which could be seen as the implementation community's version of "strict constructionism" in legal circles, has the advantage of removing some ambiguity regarding how to set benchmarks for evaluating peace operations. The Dayton text, *as a text,* would then set the defining criteria for success. Although this approach would still require some interpretation, questions of signatories' intent and subsequent interpretation would be relatively de-emphasized.[1] However, this method has serious limitations. Even within specific annexes, the Dayton text has its ambiguities, requiring extratextual interpretation: Annex 3, for example, calls for verification of "politically neutral" conditions in order to hold elections, the content of which is left open to the judgment of implementers. Moreover, the GFAP only minimally describes strategic linkages *among* its annexes: how these have related to one another in practice is demonstrably central to the Dayton project but is not particularly evident in the GFAP text. In addition, a textual approach reinforces what has often been seen as a common weakness of UN peace operations: namely, to treat their textual mandate, usually in the form of a Security Council resolution, as a set of constraints rather than as a framework of opportunities. Derek Boothby, formerly Deputy Transitional Administrator in Eastern Slavonia, describes this syndrome as treating mandates as a "ceiling" rather than a "floor," an approach that is even more problematic when one takes into account the much-discussed frailties of Security Council mandates. Furthermore, a textual approach neglects what may be a wide array of important tacit agreements and expectations among parties and implementers, established but not scripted during the course of negotiating a peace agreement.

A contrasting approach to determining objectives is to emphasize the intent of Dayton's signatories and mediators, in effect, to try to identify the parties' endgame and the relationship of the GFAP's provisions to it. Although this method may be an essential supplement to a text-based approach, it also has limitations. First, it is a highly speculative enterprise for any analyst—as well as for on-the-ground implementers—to interpret intent beyond its textual expression.[2] Second, for this reason among others, there have been seriously divergent interpretations among major implementers of what Dayton implementation should operationally entail. Third, not only have there been discontinuities among implementers in crafting their own organizational mandate within the overall context of the GFAP, but also their respective translations of the GFAP into policy for the peace operation have shifted over time. Furthermore, such adaptations that have been driven by practical obstacles and events on the ground have borne varying relationships to an overall strategy for Dayton implementation. Therefore, in engaging in evaluation, analysts need to make very clear the objectives and benchmarks for assessment that they are utilizing, since ambiguity among precisely these is one of the main challenges to implementation in practice.

In *Peacebuilding as Politics*, Elizabeth Cousens argues that there is an implicit hierarchy of goals in peace operations, the relative priority among which must be explicitly considered and debated in each particular context. In her view, postconflict peacebuilding for civil wars should give primacy to the following three objectives: first, securing a viable and sustainable cease-fire; second, creating or facilitating the conditions necessary for internal conflict resolution, which she terms "self-sustaining peace"; and third, concluding the international peace presence in a country in such a way that normalization of domestic affairs can occur.[3] She proposes that the priority given by implementers to other dimensions of peace operations, including long-term democratization and postwar justice, should be determined by their demonstrable relationship to the primary goals of effective peace and internal resilience against the resumption of conflict. Once the international community has embarked upon a peace operation, her assumption is that a minimum level of security for a new postwar state and for the population at large is a sine qua non for any more ambitious objectives in postwar political development. According to this line of reasoning, those who advocate a different set of priorities should show how any other objectives will prevent large-scale armed violence from resuming in post–civil war situations.

If one accepts this argument, then successful peace implementation in Bosnia would entail, first, securing a sustained cease-fire that can deepen into postwar stability; second, establishing the conditions necessary for a self-sustaining peace; and third, providing for the exit or significant downsizing of the international presence in Bosnia. Even these basic criteria need to be tempered, however, by an assessment of the "degree of difficulty" of the Bosnian peace operation. According to a scale of difficulty proposed by George Downs and Stephen Stedman, Bosnia occupies a middle ground of difficulty compared to other peace operations of the 1990s: easier than cases such as Liberia, Sierra Leone, Angola, Rwanda, and Somalia; but harder than cases such as El Salvador, Guatemala, Namibia, and Nicaragua.[4]

Even the three-part criteria for evaluation that we propose, admittedly, begs many questions. To argue the importance of establishing conditions favorable to internal conflict resolution is only the first and easiest step. Identifying what those conditions are, how they relate to the provisions of a peace agreement, and how international actors can help foster them is the challenge and, we argue, should be the central task of any implementation project. Evaluating Dayton implementation in these terms, then, requires some explanation of how the various military and civilian components of implementation relate to this still-elusive goal of self-sustaining peace in Bosnia. As the *Report of the Panel on United Nations Peace Operations* states: "In such complex peace operations, peacekeepers work to maintain a secure local environment while peacebuilders work to make that environment self-sustaining. Only such an environment offers a ready exit to peacekeeping forces, making peacekeepers and peacebuilders inseparable partners."[5] Only through understanding how the numerous peacekeeping and peace-building components of Dayton implementation relate to one another and to three central goals (i.e., cessation of armed violence, self-sustaining peace, and international exit) can the efficacy of the peace operation as a whole be responsibly assessed.

IMPACT AND CONSEQUENCES

Achievements

The most significant and obvious success of Dayton implementation has been the consolidation of the cease-fire that was first established on 12 October 1995 (about five weeks before the initialing of the GFAP at Dayton, Ohio, on 21 November 1995). The official transfer of authority from UNPROFOR to the NATO-led IFOR on 20 December 1995 has since been followed by a complete absence of large-scale armed conflict. IFOR, a deployment of approximately 60,000 troops, and its significantly downsized replacement, SFOR, have thus secured peace among the three Bosnian militaries where previous efforts had failed. Given the size and capabilities of these NATO-led operations, one might wonder with hindsight whether this accomplishment would ever have been in doubt. Yet if one recalls the debate at the time, including fierce rhetoric about exit strategies, it is clear that the fielding of an international force robust enough to guarantee and deepen the cease-fire was never a foregone conclusion. To ensure the U.S. military participation on which the contribution of other NATO allies depended required a fight within the U.S. administration and between the administration and Congress so arduous that it left "deep scars in the back," according to one senior official heavily involved.[6] As some other countries and peace operations have unfortunately experienced, the costs of a recurrence of conflict can be nearly incomprehensible—often resulting in even more casualties than the initial war.[7] The fact that Bosnia has avoided anything like this fate is an incontrovertible and laudable achievement of Dayton implementation.

Management of Bosnia's displaced populations has also notably improved—in particular since 1999. Although minority returns have still not occurred on a particularly large scale, and multiethnicity has generally not been effectively fostered in Bosnia, freedom of movement has been undeniably enhanced. Illegal checkpoints have been removed, transportation networks have been reestablished, and other obstacles such as nationality-coded license plates have been abolished. After its first years of essentially unsuccessful efforts to promote ethnic reintegration, the international community began to shift strategies and has now centered its approach on establishing a legal environment of nondiscrimination and protection and promoting freedom of choice for individual displaced persons. Arguably, this strategic shift has recently improved the prospects for displaced persons in Bosnia, including among potential minority return populations. In addition, at least 550,000 Bosnians have exercised their rights as refugees by choosing to remain abroad—accepting durable solutions such as asylum or third-country resettlement, which has been enabled by host countries upholding the legal principle of *nonrefoulement*.[8] Moreover, contrary to the conventional wisdom that repatriation of refugees is a necessary ingredient of successful peace implementation, refugees remaining *outside* Bosnia have arguably helped maintain stability *inside* Bosnia because their absence has commensurately reduced demand for scarce jobs, housing, and other resources.[9] Importantly, if one compares Bosnia's return process to other situations of mass displacement—for example, Cyprus or Palestine—then international return efforts in Bosnia may be considered a qualified success.

Although economic recovery in Bosnia has not yet met expectations, there are positive developments worth noting. During its transition from war to peace, the country has steadily moved from dependence upon emergency humanitarian aid to a process of economic development, though this remains, in turn, heavily dependent upon other forms of international assistance.[10] Likewise, in its transition from socialism to capitalism, Bosnia has begun to develop a legal and regulatory framework that may eventually promote a free market economy. To evaluate Bosnia's economic performance, the country should properly be compared to other postwar and postcommunist societies. According to comparative macroeconomic indicators for twenty-seven central and eastern European countries, Bosnia ranked as follows in 1998: twenty-first in GDP, seventeenth in GDP per capita, seventh in consumer price inflation, and first in GDP growth per year.[11] Although these standings are not indicative of stellar economic performance and are skewed somewhat by low postwar economic benchmarks and large infusions of international funds, they nonetheless could be construed as respectable results for a country undergoing two major transitions at once.

There has also been some progress on the democratization front.

First, elections have been held on a regular basis in Bosnia since the war ended: general elections in September 1996, September 1998, and November 2000; municipal elections in September 1997 and April 2000; and a special election in Republika Srpska in November 1997. Although conducting largely free and fair elections on a routine basis is not *sufficient* evidence of democratization, it is a necessary component of the process. Second, there have also been achievements in fostering the rule of law, notably in areas of judicial reform and institutional capacity building. Many of the problems still faced by Bosnia's courts are not unique to Bosnia or even countries in transition: inadequate staffing, case backlog, and alleged corruption can trouble even the best court systems of the industrialized democracies. Third, after IFOR's initial reluctance and IPTF's early inability to support human rights monitoring and enforcement, both IFOR's successor SFOR and IPTF have shown a greater commitment to support human rights implementation. Finally, the ICTY has arguably become more effective—particularly with respect to the apprehension and trial of persons indicted for war crimes, even though ICTY only partly addresses the broader need for mechanisms to establish accountability and justice.

Returning to our proposed criteria for evaluation, only the first— consolidating the cease-fire of 12 October 1995—has been significantly fulfilled to date. The second and third—fostering conditions for self-sustaining peace and the prospect of timely international exit—have been a disappointment. Moreover, even the cease-fire so ably stabilized by IFOR is not self-sustaining and thus requires the continuing military presence of SFOR. Residual military and public insecurity remains and, in combination with the continued power of nationalist parties, suggests that peace might not last long if the international presence was significantly downsized in the near term. Hence, more than five years after Dayton, the international community still maintains a formidable security presence as well as an expansive civilian administration. The following discussion explores some of the tactical errors, strategic miscalculations, and policy tensions that have contributed to what appears likely to remain a "permanent presence" of international involvement in postwar Bosnia.

Barriers to Greater Progress

From the beginning, the international community has relied upon a balance-of-power strategy for long-term maintenance of military security between the two entities. We argue that this was a strategic mistake. First, in the effort to bolster the military capacity of the Bosniacs (primarily) and Croats (secondarily) as a deterrent against future aggression by the army of Republika Srpska, the train and equip program of military assistance may have gone too far. As many analysts have argued, by giving the latest in NATO equipment and training to the Federation forces and creating a distinctly superior military capacity, the main accomplishment of the program has been to replace the risk of a Serb offensive with the risk of a Bosniac one. Perhaps in ethical and political terms, depending on one's loyalties, this is a welcome result, but in terms of peace implementation, it is a highly problematic one.[12] Although the risk has likely diminished compared to a few years ago, fear of a Bosniac military initiative is plausible. The Bosniacs are numerically superior and, more than the other parties to the war, consider themselves inadequately compensated by the territorial division agreed upon at Dayton. As earlier described, they were also militarily frustrated by having to stop short of a likely victory in western Bosnia, and the overall result has been an obviously unwieldy map. Although proponents of the train and equip program portray the effort as an initiative designed to enhance military cooperation and interforce confidence, it has yet to be perceived as such by the Serbs. Further, although the program has not violated the letter of the law stipulated in the Florence Agreement on regional arms control, it has certainly compromised the spirit of the pact. It also has yet to bear significant fruit in terms of integrating Bosniac and Croat forces on the Federation side.

Public security, or its lack, also contributes heavily to the continuing dependence of Bosnia's peace on an international presence. A number of terms have been used to describe this issue, variously referred to as a lack of capacity for "enforcement of human rights," a "law enforcement gap," and an "absence of ethnic security."[13] Regardless of terminology, the cease-fire among Bosnia's three armies was not effectively extended to include protection for civilian populations, especially in the early years of implementation. Although IFOR and SFOR had both the mandate and the operational capacity to prevent or respond to violence against civilian populations, whether by taking decisive steps against Bosnian paramilitaries and special police or by establishing area security in particularly volatile contexts, they have largely refrained from this responsibility or accepted it late in the day.[14] Meanwhile, the IPTF, which monitors and trains Bosnia's police forces, had neither the mandate nor the capacity to effectively prevent further human rights violations. Some tactical adjustments have been made, notably when armed Multinational Specialized Units were introduced under SFOR command to help fill the security gap between SFOR and IPTF. However, early inaction among military implementers set a decisive tone for the ensuing years of the peace operation. Public security has still not been adequately established for Bosnia's civilian population, and even where it has been accomplished, much damage had already been done. Unsurprisingly, public insecurity negatively affects the possibilities for a self-sustaining peace—particularly those aspects of international strategy dependent upon the interrelated tasks of returning Bosnia's displaced populations and promoting political moderation.

Indeed, UNHCR and other international actors made wildly optimistic predictions about the magnitude of refugee and IDP return that would occur in the first few years of Dayton implementation, only to belatedly come to terms with the serious obstacles hampering this process. Ironically, many of the impediments to returning Bosnia's displaced populations have stemmed not from intransigent nationalist elites but from decisions about how to manage basic dilemmas of implementation. The emphasis on rapid physical reconstruction in the Federation required working through existing channels of authority and may have further empowered politicians and bureaucrats hostile to Dayton's integrationist goals. Most importantly, the severe political conditionality directed at Republika Srpska led to at least a two-year delay of economic recovery in the entity. Because of the relative lack of jobs, housing, and social welfare benefits in RS compared to the Federation, most IDPs and refugees (particularly potential minority returns) were understandably averse to going back to RS. During the first two years of the peace operation, only 2,219 displaced Bosniacs and Croats returned to their prewar home of origin in Republika Srpska.[15] Thus, although imposing political conditionality on Republika Srpska was apparently intended to induce Dayton compliance, it has actually had the unintended consequence of undermining the international community's initial strategy of promoting political moderation through facilitating demographic shifts toward multiethnicity.

However, because the GFAP contains a number of provisions that are extremely problematic, one could also plausibly argue that the democratization project was doomed before it began. The agreement sets up a constitutional structure so that candidates would be elected by one entity or another but not by a statewide electoral base. Thus, ethnonational politics are essentially intrinsic within the GFAP. Furthermore, the agreement promised that voters would be allowed to vote in constituencies where they *intend* to live, stipulated that the first election would be held within the first six to nine months of implementation, and predicted that the return of Bosnia's displaced persons would have been well under way by then. As noted above, the GFAP was very wrong on this last point. Nonetheless, under heavy pressure from the United States (among others), the OSCE reluctantly allowed elections to go ahead in September 1996—even though the conditions were hardly ideal for a truly "free and fair" ballot. Bosnia's voters, faced with a measure of physical insecurity and a particularly uncertain future, understandably voted for nationalist politicians who (if nothing else) had consistently promised to protect their own ethnicity's interests. This vote, which consolidated wartime leaders' hold on power, has had a decidedly negative impact upon efforts to facilitate a self-sustaining peace. Ever since the first general election, the international community has faced an uphill climb on a virtual Mt. Igman of nationalist politics at least partly of its own making.

ASSESSMENT

To say the least, organizations tasked with implementing Dayton, along with supporting governments, faced an exceedingly difficult challenge. The cease-fire of October 1995 and ensuing negotiations at Dayton had only been accomplished through heavy third-party coercion, including UN-authorized sanctions, NATO air strikes, and an externally well-trained and equipped Bosniac-Croat ground offensive. Significantly, neither the Bosnian Croat nor the Bosnian Serb leadership were actually signatories of the GFAP. The Bosnian Serbs, who had recently sustained considerable battlefield losses along with their allies in the Krajina region of Croatia, were represented at Dayton by their patron in Belgrade, Slobodan Milosevic.[16] Likewise, the Bosnian Croats were represented not by their own local leadership, but by their sponsor in Zagreb, Franjo Tudjman. Having had no real participation in the negotiations, Bosnian Croat and Serb leadership were unsurprisingly hostile to a wide range of subsequent implementation efforts, and perhaps their patrons wanted it that way. Furthermore, although Izetbegovic represented the Bosniacs at the talks, many Bosniacs felt cheated on the crucial issue of territorial allocation, even while recognizing the extraordinary pressure being exerted on Izetbegovic by the United States to sign. Finally, because of the Bosnian leadership's strong opposition to proposed integrationist provisions, the GFAP barely contained its strategic contradictions. Hence, from the first day of Dayton implementation, there have been nearly irreconcilable tensions among the substantial power given to the entities, the right of return promised to displaced persons, and the legal sovereignty and responsibilities accorded an ostensibly unitary Bosnian state.

Ironically, issues of power imbalance and the tension between central coordination and decentralized authority are also present within the international community. Lead agencies in implementation were essentially given full creative control within their assigned responsibilities, with any broader coordination to be developed on the ground. Most destructively, Dayton stipulated a strict segregation between military and civilian components of the accord, at the insistence of the United States.[17] Hence, the commanders of IFOR and SFOR were in no way accountable to the OHR or even the PIC or the UN Security Council, but rather to the North Atlantic Council in Brussels. The ensuing absence of adequate civilian-military coordination has posed serious problems for issues arguably at the heart of successful implementation in Bosnia, in particular, provision of public security, the return of displaced persons, and the democratization of politics.[18] Further complicating matters, OHR never enjoyed effective coordinating capacity over civilian agencies either.[19] Over time, discontinuities on the civilian side became problematic enough and public enough that greater political support among capitals was marshaled behind OHR through the PIC. Meanwhile, OHR has also established multiple bodies and mechanisms to coordinate various aspects of civilian implementation, though these have often lacked effective operational capacity to coordinate.[20] What is questionable is whether the ground lost in the first two years of implementation can be regained.

A related and persistent problem has been that the roles of international actors were allocated significantly on the basis of institutional and national bargaining rather than comparative advantage.[21] Simply put, mandates were assigned and tasks were assumed less based on who could do the job best than on which agencies and states were favored at Dayton. For example, the OSCE was mandated to run elections in Bosnia even though it had no prior experience in this area. The UN, which *did* have significant electoral experience, was seen as discredited in Bosnia by the UNPROFOR experience. What was more decisive, the United States enjoyed greater leverage within the OSCE and could count on an approach to implementation with which it was comfortable and that matched its ostensible schedule for military exit from Bosnia at the end of 1996. Furthermore, in the one area where the United Nations was given authority, police monitoring and reform, it was burdened with weaknesses typical to CIVPOL operations and with drastically insufficient resources in a context in which public security could be expected to be an early and serious challenge. (However, it is hard to identify an organization that would not have faced these same difficulties.)

Domestic political considerations among Dayton's supporting governments also weighed heavily on events in Bosnia—usually with distinctly negative implications for the success of the peace operation as a whole. Although there are many examples, one issue clearly had the most impact on Dayton implementation: the perceived need for the Clinton administration to publicly commit to an exit strategy with a predetermined date of departure in order to gain congressional support for the Bosnian operation. For example, when Secretary of Defense William Perry and Secretary of State Warren Christopher testified at the House International Relations Committee on 18 October 1995, they repeatedly and explicitly reassured the members that U.S. troops would be committed for only one year.[22] However, public pronouncements of exit strategies and timelines can do heavy damage to the prospects for a successful peace operation.[23] In particular, the U.S. preoccupation with announcing how and when the NATO-led force would *leave* Bosnia virtually assured that IFOR (or its successor, SFOR) would need to *stay* much longer than initially anticipated. Although exit strategies may have played well with a relatively isolationist Congress and with the 1996 presidential election looming only one year ahead, they also encouraged those parties hostile to Dayton to just "wait out" what would supposedly be a short-lived international military presence. Consequently, there was very little early progress in implementing Dayton's integrationist provisions, and it does not appear—even after more than five years of implementation—that NATO will be leaving Bosnia anytime soon.

On the issue of reunification, Bosnia is still de facto three nations and two states within one de jure nation-state. Hence, disappointed with the pace and trajectory of developments, the international community has increasingly resorted to the use of its own authority, largely through OHR, to impose decisions in a Bosnian political context. In late 1997, the Peace Implementation Council granted OHR its "Bonn powers," which include the right to dismiss public officials and issue binding decisions by decree. Since then, OHR has used this authority to establish a number of common institutions.[24] Unfortunately, OHR has also resorted to its Bonn powers to dismiss democratically elected officials, including RS president Nikola Poplasen in March 1999, who apparently obstructed Dayton implementation. This is a troubling precedent for the international community, not least because resort to OHR power may undermine both indigenous democratization and the legitimacy of the international community's presence in Bosnia. The exercise of international authority to unify Bosnia thus remains both contradictory and self-perpetuating: the more it is used to combat perceived obstructionism, the more enmeshed international actors become in Bosnia's domestic political life. This is a persistent dilemma between intervention and sovereignty with which the international community has yet to come to terms in Bosnia.

NOTES

1. A very strong example of this approach is the periodic Dayton "report card" issued by the International Crisis Group. Its 1999 report, *Is Dayton Failing? Bosnia Four Years After the Peace Agreement*, has been very useful as a scorecard of Dayton annex by annex. However, its overall analytical insights are also constrained by its structural reliance upon mirroring the text of the peace agreement itself.

2. This is one of the central issues addressed by Donald Rothchild, "The Nexus Between Mediation and Implementation," in Stephen John Stedman, Donald Rothchild, and Elizabeth M. Cousens, eds., "Strategies, Organizations, and Consequences: Explaining the Outcome of Peace Implementation in Civil Wars," vol. 2 of "Ending Civil Wars," a joint research project of the Center for International Security and Cooperation and the Peace Academy, unpublished manuscript.

3. Elizabeth Cousens, "Introduction," in Elizabeth Cousens and Chetan Kumar, with Karin Wermester, eds., *Peacebuilding as Politics: Cultivating Peace in Fragile Societies* (Boulder, CO: Lynne Rienner Publishers, 2000).

4. See George Downs and Stephen John Stedman, "Evaluating the Implementation of Peace Agreements," in Stephen John Stedman, Donald Rothchild, and Elizabeth M. Cousens, eds., "Strategies, Organizations, and Consequences: Explaining the Outcome of Peace Implementation in Civil Wars," vol. 2 of "Ending Civil Wars," a joint research project of the Center for International Security and Cooperation and the Peace Academy, unpublished manuscript. According to their methodology, which is based on nine factors, the most difficult peace operations would have a high "conflict score" (two or more parties, disposable resources, no peace agreement, collapsed state, likely spoilers, and more than 50,000 soldiers) and a low third-party "willingness score" (great-power interest, resource commitment, and ability to risk lives).

5. United Nations, *Report of the Panel on United Nations Peace Operations*, 21 August 2000, A/55/305–S/2000/809, pp. viii–ix.

6. Confidential remark to author, October 1998.

7. The failure of the United Nations Verification Mission II (UNAVEM II) to prevent the resumption of war in Angola (1992–1994) cost the lives of approximately 300,000 people, probably more than the total number killed from sixteen previous years of civil war; and the breakdown of implementation of the Arusha Accords in Rwanda ushered in a genocide that cost nearly 1 million lives. On Angola, see Human Rights Watch, *Angola Unravels: The Rise and Fall of the Lusaka Peace Process* (New York: Human Rights Watch, 1999), p. 15. On Rwanda, see Bruce D. Jones, *Peacemaking in Rwanda: The Dynamics of Failure* (Boulder, CO: Lynne Rienner Publishers, forthcoming).

8. *Nonrefoulement,* the principle that refugees cannot be forcibly returned to their country of origin, is the central tenet of international refugee law.

9. This is particularly true when one considers that most of these refugees would have added to the ranks of Bosnia's internally displaced persons had they chosen repatriation instead of asylum or third-country resettlement. Some U.S. NGOs engaging in third-country resettlement of Bosnian refugees have explicitly recognized as much in their planning and have argued for higher resettlement admissions on these grounds.

10. Notably, interentity commercial ties were among the first to be reestablished after the war—with buyers, sellers, and traders flocking to informal markets (e.g. the "Arizona market") along the ZOS—though this occurred spontaneously and independently of any international assistance. In fact, at an early stage, IFOR particularly worried about these spontaneous markets as potential security risks.

11. Economist Intelligence Unit, *Country Profile: Bosnia and Herzegovina 1999–2000* (London: Economist Intelligence Unit).

12. See, for example, Charles G. Boyd, "Making Bosnia Work," *Foreign Affairs* (January–February 1998): 42–55; Jane M. O. Sharp, "Dayton Report Card," *International Security* 22, no. 3 (winter 1997–1998): 101–137.

13. Phrases used by Manfred Nowak, Jane M. O. Sharp, and the International Crisis Group, respectively.

14. The typical response by military commanders was that these responsibilities were part of Dayton's civilian provisions. This problem was much worse with IFOR than with its successor.

15. In this book, see Table 4.3, "Minority Returns to and Within Bosnia 1996–1999," p. 79.

16. There has been much speculation about exactly how and why Milosevic managed to deliver the acquiescence of the Bosnian Serbs, but the comprehensive sanctions regime in place against Yugoslavia probably had something to do with prompting him to strong-arm Karadzic and Mladic into accepting Dayton's terms. See "Sanctioning Yugoslavia," pp. 63–86 in David Cortright and George A. Lopez, *The Sanctions Decade: Assessing UN Strategies in the 1990s* (Boulder, CO: Lynne Rienner Publishers, 2000).

17. After the problems experienced by UNPROFOR with the "dual-key" military command structure during the war, the United States has since refused to put its troops under the direct authority of UN civilian personnel.

18. Michael C. Williams, *Civil-Military Relations and Peacekeeping*, Adelphi Paper no. 321 (London: International Institute for Strategic Studies, 1998); George Joulwan and Christopher C. Shoemaker, *Civilian-Military Cooperation in the Prevention of Deadly Conflict: Implementing Agreements in Bosnia and Beyond* (New York: Carnegie Commission on Preventing Deadly Conflict, December 1998).

19. In this book, see Figure 2.1, "Relationships Among Major Implementing Agencies," p. 42.

20. As an example, see Michael O' Flaherty's critique of OHR's Human Rights Coordinating Center, "International Human Rights Operations in Bosnia and Herzegovina," pp. 71–96 in Alice H. Henkin, ed., *Honoring Human Rights: From Peace to Justice* (Washington, DC: Aspen Institute, 1998).

21. Georgios Kostakos, "Division of Labor Among International Organizations: The Bosnian Experience," *Global Governance* 4, no. 1 (October–December 1998): 461–484.

22. Perry stated that the "implementation force will complete its mission

in a period not to exceed 12 months," and Christopher testified that U.S. troops would "remain for a limited period of time—approximately one year."

23. See, for example, Gideon Rose, "Exit Strategy Delusion," *Foreign Affairs* (January–February 1998): 56–67.

24. For example, currency and coinage, flag, anthem, citizenship standards, vehicle license plates, border service, and electoral regulations.

10

Conclusion

If considered in broad terms, the Bosnian experience contains multiple lessons for peace operations elsewhere and highlights areas requiring further research. Here, we briefly identify four areas in need of additional and sustained attention: organizational reform; the constraints imposed on peace operations by domestic politics in intervening countries; criteria for entry and exit strategies; and the relationship between sovereignty and international authority in postconflict peacebuilding.

There is a need for more research and new policy initiatives on reforming the way in which international organizations conduct their "peace operations." Issues of structure, division of labor, monitoring, reporting, accountability, and governance need exploration. Peace operations should be structured according to relative merit and comparative advantage rather than narrow institutional and state interests. Also, strategic coordination, although clearly required, is often regrettably absent. Thus, lines of authority need to be more clearly delineated and more pragmatically designed for the particularly difficult circumstances faced by peace operations. Furthermore, mechanisms should be developed for systematically setting benchmarks and criteria for evaluating both the efficacy and ethics of intervention. More broadly, some institutional accountability among international organizations and states implementing peace operations needs to be instilled. In particular, this means more democratic, transparent governance *within* international organizations and state agencies.[1] Although more open governance within implementing agencies will not solve all the dilemmas faced in peace operations, it would be a helpful step toward improving performance and accountability in international peace implementation efforts.

Another important issue concerns how domestic politics affects the conduct of foreign policy in general and peace operations in particular.

Can stamina be developed, or will international peace interventions always be vulnerable to isolationist strains in key states? Can the media help overcome such reservations, which may require greater effort to communicate the complexities and dilemmas of peace operations? It is readily apparent that the domestic politics of intervening countries are a crucial factor in determining the ultimate viability of a protracted peace operation. Perhaps some lessons have already been learned on this front.

There also could be far more serious consideration of "entry strategies." Devising and embarking upon an appropriate international role in peace implementation should take into account the types of challenges likely to be encountered in a particular operation, including such factors as security vacuums and likely spoilers, simultaneous transitions of regime or economic system, and the strategic treatment of civilians and communities by former belligerents. A proper entry strategy must also assess the genuine capacity, or its absence, in international response. This entails considering such factors as willingness and capacity to use coercion, likelihood of organizational competition instead of cooperation, specific domestic political constraints, and the broader level of commitment by key states. Such considerations may face the international community with tough but very basic choices: to scale down the goals and modalities of a peace operation to meet the available "supply" of international resources or to invigorate its efforts to overcome obstacles should the "demand" of a particular peace operation be sufficiently high. The latter may be strategically—and often ethically—preferable to the former, but it requires a marshaling of international resources and a unity of effort among international actors that is extremely difficult to attain.

In turn, one has to give explicit attention to goals, evaluation, and exit. Here, we have proposed that a self-enforcing cease-fire is necessary for an international exit on minimalist grounds, while self-sustaining peace is needed for more credible drawing down of international engagement.

Both academics and practitioners also need better to grapple with the implications of the increasing reliance on regimes of international authority to accomplish state building. Cambodia may have begun the trend, but Bosnia took it to a new level, which Kosovo and East Timor have, in some fashion, followed. In Bosnia, the international community got off to a particularly slow start with some aspects of Dayton implementation and then subsequently tried to make up for this shortfall by increasingly imposing decisions by decree in the political sphere. In our view, had OHR and other actors possessed *and used wisely* a stronger mandate in the first few years, there would be far less need now for the kind of heavy-handed intervention that seems unlikely to subside soon. Our concern is that an international override of sovereignty in order eventually to build it, runs a high risk of being counterproductive and, in particular, jeopardizing the further goal of restoring normalcy to postwar societies.

Members of the international community are presently engaged in trying to learn lessons in real time as they embark on other operations. The most direct application of learning from Bosnia, independent of whether the right lessons have been identified, has been in Kosovo—yet Bosnia's lessons extend far beyond just that case. Dayton implementation was the largest peace operation of the 1990s. It has, for better or worse, played a crucial role in defining the post–Cold War role for the North Atlantic Treaty Organization, the Organization for Security and Cooperation in Europe, the European Union, and the United Nations— as well as for states such as Germany, the United Kingdom, France, and the United States. In our view, grappling with the political and organizational determinants of the successes and failures of Dayton implementation is important for a multilateral community that is extended widely and deeply in conflict zones from East Timor to the Democratic Republic of Congo. Making mistakes is easy; overcompensating for them is tempting. Getting international peace efforts right at the outset may require difficult reflection within the international community about its manifest limits. It is, however, indispensable.

NOTE

1. See, for example, Ngaire Woods, "Good Governance in International Organizations," *Global Governance* (January–March 1999): 39–62.

Appendix 1

Abbreviations and Acronyms

ABiH	Army of Bosnia and Herzegovina
ACV	armored combat vehicle
AFP	Agence France Presse
BiH	Bosnia and Herzegovina
CAFAO	Customs and Fiscal Assistance Office
CIVPOL	civilian police
COMIFOR	Commander, Implementation Force
COMSFOR	Commander, Stabilization Force
CRPC	Commission for Real Property Claims of Displaced Persons and Refugees
EASC	Election Appeals Sub-Commission
EC	European Community
ECCY	European Community Conference on the Former Yugoslavia
ESI	European Stability Initiative
EU	European Union
FBiH	Federation of Bosnia and Herzegovina
FDI	foreign direct investment
FRY	Federal Republic of Yugoslavia
G-7/8	Group of Seven/Eight
GAO	General Accounting Office
GDP	gross domestic product
GFAP	General Framework Agreement for Peace in Bosnia and Herzegovina
HDZ	Croatian Democratic Union
HRCC	Human Rights Coordination Center
HVO	Croatian Defense Force
ICC	International Criminal Court

ICFY	International Conference on the Former Yugoslavia
ICG	International Crisis Group
ICRC	International Committee of the Red Cross
ICTR	International Criminal Tribunal for Rwanda
ICTY	International Criminal Tribunal for Yugoslavia
IEBL	Inter-Entity Boundary Line
IFIs	international financial institutions
IFOR	Implementation Force
IISS	International Institute for Strategic Studies
IMC	Independent Media Commission
IMF	International Monetary Fund
IPA	International Peace Academy
IPTF	International Police Task Force
IRC	International Rescue Committee
JMC	Joint Military Commission
JNA	Yugoslav National Army
KM	konvertible marka
MEC	Media Experts Commission
MPRI	Military Professional Resources Incorporated
MSU	Multinational Specialized Unit
NAC	North Atlantic Council
NATO	North Atlantic Treaty Organization
NERIC	National Election Results Implementation Committee
NGOs	nongovernmental organizations
OCI	Open Cities Initiative
OHR	Office of the High Representative
OSCE	Organization for Security and Cooperation in Europe
PEC	Provisional Election Commission
PIC	Peace Implementation Council
PIFWC	person indicted for war crimes
PLIP	Property Law Implementation Plan
PRRP	Priority Reconstruction and Recovery Program
RFE/RL	Radio Free Europe/Radio Liberty
RRTF	Reconstruction and Return Task Force
RS	Republika Srpska
SACEUR	Supreme Allied Commander in Europe
SDA	Party for Democratic Action
SDS	Serb Democratic Party
SFOR	Stabilization Force
SRS	Serb Radical Party
SRSG	Special Representative of the Secretary-General
UN	United Nations

UNAVEM II	United Nations Verification Mission II
UNESCO	United Nations Educational, Scientific, and Cultural Organization
UNHCHR	United Nations High Commissioner for Human Rights
UNHCR	United Nations High Commissioner for Refugees
UNMIBH	United Nations Mission in Bosnia and Herzegovina
UNPAs	United Nations Protected Areas
UNPROFOR	United Nations Protection Force
UNTAES	United Nations Transitional Administration for Eastern Slavonia, Baranja, and Western Sirmium
USAID	U.S. Agency for International Development
USCR	United States Committee for Refugees
VJ	Army of Yugoslavia
VRS	Army of Republika Srpska
ZOS	Zone of Separation

Appendix 2

Chronology

1946	State of Yugoslavia is established, with six republics and two autonomous provinces.
1954	Serbo-Croatian is officially recognized as one language.
1974	Yugoslavia's third constitution devolves greater autonomy to republics as well as establishes for Muslims constitutional status as a sixth official nationality.
1980	Josip Broz Tito dies.
1989	
28 February	The first public meeting of HDZ is held in Croatia.
March	Yugoslavia's constitution is amended to limit the autonomy of Serbia's two autonomous provinces, Kosovo and Vojvodina.
28 June	One million Serbs travel to see Milosevic deliver nationalist speech in Kosovo.
27 September	Slovenia declares itself "sovereign and independent state."
1990	
17 February	SDS founded in Croatia.
April	Slovenia holds democratic elections, the first among Yugoslavia's republics to do so.
May	In democratic elections in Croatia, the nationalist party wins, and Tudjman is elected president.
26 May	SDA founded, with Izetbegovic as president of party.

July	Bosnian SDS founded, with Karadzic as president of party; Bosnian HDZ founded.
November	In democratic elections in Bosnia, nationalist parties win.
December	In democratic elections in Serbia, Milosevic is elected president.

1991

25 June	Slovenia and Croatia declare independence.
27 June	Armed conflict begins in Slovenia.

1992

January	In anticipation of war, the JNA transfers Bosnian Serbs back to Bosnian territory.
9 January	Bosnian Serbs declare Serbian Republika BiH (later Republika Srpska).
15 January	The EC recognizes Slovenia and Croatia as independent states.
21 February	The Security Council establishes UNPROFOR with initial twelve-month mandate.
6 April	The EC and United States recognize Bosnia as an independent state.
mid-April	Serb forces occupy two-thirds of Bosnia and one-third of Croatia.
9 October	Security Council establishes a no-fly zone over Bosnia.

1993

16 April	Security Council establishes UN Safe Area for Srebrenica.
6 May	UN Safe Areas extended to five other locations in Bosnia.
25 May	ICTY is established by the Security Council.

1994

1 March	Bosniac-Croat alliance brokered under Washington Agreement.

1995

May	NATO air strikes against Bosnian Serb forces lead to hundreds of UN peacekeepers being held hostage by Bosnian Serbs.
12 July	Srebrenica falls to Bosnian Serb forces, and thousands of Bosniacs are killed.
25 July	Radovan Karadzic and General Ratko Mladic are indicted by the ICTY.
4–6 August	Croatian army launches Operation Storm in

	Krajina and expels at least 200,000 Serb civilians and troops to Bosnia and Serbia.
28 August	Bosnian Serbs shell Sarajevo marketplace—killing thirty-seven civilians.
late August	NATO delivers air strikes against Bosnian Serb positions.
late September	Serbs lose territory to HVO and ABiH, resulting in a 51 percent HVO/ABiH to 49 percent Serb territorial split.
3 October	Erdut Agreement is reached between Serbia and Croatia, committing Serb forces to transfer of Eastern Slavonia to Croatian sovereignty.
12 October	Cease-fire declared in Bosnia and Croatia among all forces.
1–20 November	Proximity talks are held at Wright-Patterson Air Force Base in Dayton, Ohio.
21 November	The GFAP is initialed in Dayton, Ohio.
8–9 December	The PIC is established in London.
14 December	GFAP is signed by Milosevic, Tudjman, and Izetbegovic in Paris.
20 December	UNPROFOR transfers authority to NATO-led IFOR.
21–22 December	The first Brussels donor conference is boycotted by the RS delegation.

1996

mid-January	The first meetings of major implementation agencies, the Joint Civilian Commission, and the Joint Interim Commission are held; all are chaired by High Representative Carl Bildt.
1 February	The first meeting of the PEC is held, chaired by OSCE (Robert Frowick, Head of Mission).
March	Approximately 60,000 Serb residents leave Sarajevo for RS and Yugoslavia, when Serb suburbs are transferred to Federation authority.
21 March	The first meeting of the CRPC is held.
13 April	The second Brussels donor conference takes place.
13–14 June	A PIC meeting in Florence leads to Florence Agreement on Sub-Regional Arms Control.
28–29 June	The G-7/8 Lyon summit demands that Karadzic leave political office.
30 June	Karadzic notifies Bildt he will resign, Biljana

	Plavsic is designated acting president of Republika Srpska.
18 July	Richard Holbrooke brokers a deal with Karadzic to step down as president of Republika Srpska and refrain from public political activities.
19 July	The BiH election campaign begins.
27 August	OSCE announces the first postponement of municipal elections.
31 August	The formal deadline arrives for dissolution of Bosnian Croat "Herceg-Bosna."
14 September	The first round of statewide elections is held for BiH presidency, BiH House of Representatives, RS presidency, RS National Assembly, Federation House of Representatives, and Federation canton assemblies.
29 September	PEC certifies the results: Alija Izetbegovic, Kresimir Zubak, and Momcilo Krajisnik will form the three-member BiH presidency; Izetbegovic serves as chairman.
5 October	BiH president and BiH House of Representatives are inaugurated.
22 October	OSCE announces second postponement of municipal elections.
14 November	PIC Steering Board holds a meeting in Paris.
1 December	RS government announces it has withdrawn from the Brcko arbitration process.
2 December	IFOR mandate is extended eighteen months in form of successor SFOR; UNMIBH and IPTF mandates are extended twelve months; William Crouch named COMSFOR.
4–5 December	PIC meeting is held in London.

1997

January	The RRTF is created by OHR, UNHCR, and other agencies working with displaced persons.
10 February	Large-scale clashes between Bosniacs and Croats occur in Mostar, as Bosniacs attempt to visit graves on holy day; curfew imposed; IPTF and SFOR patrols increase.
14 February	Brcko arbitrator announces interim decision on Brcko, with postponement of final decision for at least one year and increase in IPTF presence in the city.

March	UNHCR launches OCI to promote minority returns.
6 March	OSCE announces third postponement of municipal elections until 13–14 September 1997.
7 March	Brcko Implementation Conference is held in Vienna.
2 April	PIC Steering Board meeting is held in Istanbul.
28 April	High Commissioner for Refugees Sadako Ogata announces that only those municipalities and regions that accept minority returns will receive assistance from UNHCR.
9 May	IPTF launches a new policy to remove illegal checkpoints; joint patrols begin with SFOR.
30 May	PIC Steering Board meeting held in Sintra.
12 June	Carlos Westendorp replaces Carl Bildt as High Representative.
14–17 June	In Croatian elections, Tudjman wins presidency.
late June	U.S. House of Representatives threatens to end U.S. funding for SFOR when mandate ends in June 1998.
July	Wesley Clark named new SACEUR; Eric Shinseki replaces William Crouch as COMSFOR.
1 July	Westendorp announces the appointment of Ambassador Jacques Paul Klein as new principal deputy high representative.
3 July	Republika Srpska president Plavsic orders dissolution of RS National Assembly and calls for new elections; assembly defies her instructions.
8 July	PIC meeting is held in Madrid.
23–24 July	Third Brussels donor conference takes place.
8 August	SFOR announces new inspections of entity special police forces.
15 August	Plavsic forms her own party, the Serb Popular Party.
17 August	IPTF and SFOR enter the Public Security Center in Banja Luka in response to allegations by Plavsic of human rights abuses.
28 August	Several hundred people attack the UN police station; SFOR troops fire tear gas and warning shots at Bosnian Serb demonstrators in Brcko; Serb radio transmissions blamed for inciting violence.

13–14 September	First round of municipal elections is held in Bosnia and Herzegovina.
15 September	EASC decides to annul SDS electoral victory in Pale; Robert Frowick invokes chairman's decision to overturn EASC decision.
November	International community shifts strategy on application of political conditionality to RS, and donor funds to the entity increase.
6 November	PIC Steering Board meets in Sarajevo.
22–23 November	National Assembly elections are held in RS.
9 December	Agreement on a common passport, a law for a common citizenship, and a law on the functioning of the Bosnian cabinet, with timetables for implementation, are signed by three members of the Bosnian presidency.
10 December	PIC meeting is held in Bonn.

1998

12 January	RS National Assembly session: Dragan Kalinic is reelected Assembly president, Nikola Poplasen and Jovan Mitrovic are elected as his deputies.
15 January	UNTAES mandate in Croatia ends, with full transfer of authority over Eastern Slavonia to Zagreb.
17 January	Milorad Dodik is elected prime minister.
19 January	Robert L. Barry replaces Frowick as OSCE Head of Mission.
February	Elisabeth Rehn replaces Kai Eide as SRSG for UNMIBH.
15 March	PIC Steering Board meets in Sarajevo.
17 March	Federation reforms property laws to conform to Dayton and OHR requirements.
7–8 May	Fourth Brussels donor conference is held.
1 June	OHR deadline for implementation of common license plates in Bosnia is reached.
9 June	PIC Steering Board meets in Luxembourg.
11 June	OHR creates the IMC to regulate media.
15 June	Security Council extends mandate of UNMIBH and SFOR for twelve months.
22 June	A new Bosnian currency—the konvertible marka (KM)—goes into circulation.
4 August	An MSU of armed police is created to fill security gap between SFOR and IPTF.

12–13 September	Second round of statewide elections is held.
October	Montgomery Meigs replaces Shinseki as COMS-FOR.
2 December	RS reforms property laws to conform to Dayton and OHR requirements.
9 December	Representatives of the UN and RS sign the general framework agreement on restructuring, reforming, and democratizing the RS police.
15–16 December	PIC meets in Madrid.

1999

2 February	PIC meets in Brussels.
3 March	RS president Nikola Poplasen tries to unseat RS prime minister Milorad Dodik on the basis of signatures of twenty-six members of the RS National Assembly.
5 March	OHR removes Nikola Poplasen from the office of president of RS; this action is formally approved by PEC on 8 March. Arbitral Tribunal announces Final Brcko Award; RS prime minister Dodik resigns over Brcko decision.
7 March	RS National Assembly passes resolutions rejecting the arbitration on Brcko and the High Representative's dismissal of Nikola Poplasen.
15 March	RS prime minister Milorad Dodik withdraws his resignation.
20–21 May	Fifth Brussels donor conference is held.
27 May	ICTY publicly indicts Milosevic for crimes in Kosovo.
12 July	PIC Steering Board meeting is held in Brussels; Wolfgang Petritsch is named new High Representative.
13 July	Jacques Paul Klein named new SRSG for UNMIBH.
30 July	Stability Pact for South-Eastern Europe summit is held in Sarajevo.
21 September	Commission on Citizenship convenes for the first time in Sarajevo.
October	A draft election law is proposed and is later incorporated into PEC rules and regulations; Ronald Adams replaces Montgomery Meigs as COMSFOR.
22 October	PEC denies certification of two Serb parties,

| | notably including Poplasen's SRS, for municipal elections in 2000. |
| 10 December | Franjo Tudjman, president of the Republic of Croatia, dies. |

2000

7 February	Stipe Mesic is elected president of Croatia.
23–24 March	PIC meets in Brussels.
3 April	Momcilo Krajisnik, former Serb member of Bosnian presidency, is detained by SFOR due to sealed ICTY indictment for war crimes.
8 April	Second round of municipal elections is held in Bosnia and Herzegovina.
19 May	PEC decides that the general elections in BiH will be held on 11 November 2000.
11 November	General elections are held for BiH House of Representatives, RS presidency, and RS National Assembly, Federation House of Representatives, Federation canton assemblies, and the municipality of Srebrenica.

Bibliography

SELECTED SOURCES

Adelman, Howard. "Peace Agreements: Refugee Repatriation and Reintegration." Unpublished paper, CISAC-IPA Project on Implementing Peace Agreements in Civil Wars.

Akhavan, Payam. "The Yugoslav Tribunal at a Crossroads: The Dayton Peace Agreement and Beyond." *Human Rights Quarterly* 18 (1996): 259–285.

Anstee, Margaret J. "Strengthening the Role of the Department of Political Affairs as Focal Point for Post-Conflict Peace-Building." Internal Report for the Under-Secretary-General for Political Affairs of the United Nations. New York: United Nations, 30 October 1998.

Ball, Nicole. *Making Peace Work: The Role of the International Development Community.* Washington, DC: Overseas Development Council; and Baltimore, MD: Johns Hopkins University Press, 1996.

Bass, Warren. "The Triage of Dayton." *Foreign Affairs* (September–October 1998): 95–108.

Bennett, Christopher. "Bosnia: New Opportunities." *Security Dialogue* 30, no. 3 (September 1999): 291–293.

Bertram, Eva. "Reinventing Government: The Promise and Perils of Peacebuilding." *The Journal of Conflict Resolution* 39, no. 3 (September 1995): 387–418.

Bosco, David L. "Reintegrating Bosnia: A Progress Report." *Washington Quarterly* 21, no. 2 (spring 1998): 65–81.

Boyd, Charles G. "Making Bosnia Work." *Foreign Affairs* (January–February 1998): 42–55.

Bradbury, Mark. "Behind the Rhetoric of the Relief-to-Development Continuum." Unpublished paper prepared for CARE Canada, "NGOs in Complex Emergencies Project, September 1997."

Brown, Michael E., ed. *Ethnic Conflict and International Security.* Princeton: Princeton University Press, 1993.

———. *The International Dimensions of Internal Conflict.* Cambridge, MA.: MIT, 1996.

Bugajski, Janusz, Jonathan S. Landay, John R. Lampe, Charles Lane, and

Christine Wallich. "Policy Forum: Bosnia After the Troops Leave." *Washington Quarterly* 19, no. 3 (summer 1996): 69–88.

Chandler, David. "Democratization in Bosnia: The Limits of Civil Society Building Strategies." *Democratization* 5, no. 4 (winter 1998): 78–102.

———. *Bosnia: Faking Democracy After Dayton.* London: Pluto Press, 1999.

Chopra, Jarat. *The Politics of Peace Maintenance.* Boulder, CO: Lynne Rienner Publishers, 1998.

Coker, Christopher. "How Wars End." *Millennium: Journal of International Studies* 26, no. 3, special issue (1997): 615–630.

Cortright, David, ed. *The Price of Peace: Incentives and International Conflict Prevention.* Carnegie Commission on Preventing Deadly Conflict. Lanham, MD: Rowman and Littlefield, 1997.

Cortright, David, and George A. Lopez. *The Sanctions Decade: Assessing UN Strategies in the 1990s.* Boulder, CO: Lynne Rienner Publishers, 2000.

Cousens, Elizabeth M. "Making Peace in Bosnia Work." *Cornell International Law Journal* 30, no. 3 (1997): 789–818.

———. "Introduction." In Elizabeth Cousens and Chetan Kumar, with Karin Wermester, eds., *Peacebuilding as Politics: Cultivating Peace in Fragile Societies.* Boulder, CO: Lynne Rienner Publishers, 2000.

Cousens, Elizabeth M., Donald Rothchild, and Stephen J. Stedman, eds. "Putting Peace into Practice: Implementation of Peace Agreements in Civil Wars." Vol. 1 of "Ending Civil Wars," a joint research project of the Center for International Security and Co-operation and the International Peace Academy. Unpublished manuscript.

Cox, Marcus. *Strategic Approaches to International Intervention in Bosnia and Herzegovina.* Sarajevo: Center for Applied Studies in International Negotiations, October 1998.

Crisp, Jeff. "Who Has Counted the Refugees? UNHCR and the Politics of Numbers." Working Paper no. 12. Geneva: Policy Research Unit, UNHCR, June 1999.

Crocker, Chester A., Fen Osler Hampson, and Pamela Aall, eds. *Herding Cats: Multiparty Mediation in a Complex World.* Washington, DC: United States Institute of Peace Press, 1999.

Cutts, Mark. "The Humanitarian Operation in Bosnia, 1992–1995: Dilemmas of Negotiating Humanitarian Access." Working Paper no. 8. Geneva: Policy Research Unit, UNHCR, May 1999.

Daalder, Ivo H. "Bosnia After SFOR: Options for Continued U.S. Engagement." *Survival* 39, no. 4 (winter 1997–1998): 5–28. With responses from Carl Bildt, Pauline Neville-Jones, and Robert A. Pape.

Daadler, Ivo H., and Michael B. G. Froman. "Dayton's Incomplete Peace." *Foreign Affairs* (November–December 1999): 106–113.

de Rossanet, Bertrand. *Peacemaking and Peacekeeping in Yugoslavia.* Nijhoff Law Specials, vol. 17. The Hague: Kluwer Law International, 1996.

de Soto, Alvaro, and Graçiana del Castillo. "Obstacles to Peacebuilding." *Foreign Policy* 94 (spring 1994): 69–83.

Doyle, Michael, and Nicholas Sambanis. "Strategies of Peacebuilding: A Theoretical and Quantitative Analysis." Unpublished paper, 29 September 1999.

Economist Intelligence Unit. *Country Profiles* and *Country Reports* for Bosnia-Herzegovina. London: Economic Intelligence Unit.

European Commission and World Bank. *Bosnia and Herzegovina 1996–1998: Lessons and Accomplishments: Review of the Priority Reconstruction and Recovery Program and Looking Ahead Towards Sustainable Economic Development.* May 1999. Available online at http://www.worldbank. org.ba/wbinba/blue%20book%20bosnia.pdf.

———. *Priority Reconstruction Program: Achievements and 1998 Needs.* April 1998.

European Stability Initiative Publications. Available online at http://www. esiweb.org/hauptseite.html.

Forman, Shepard, and Stewart Patrick, eds. *Good Intentions: Pledges of Aid for Postconflict Recovery.* Center on International Cooperation Studies in Multilateralism. Boulder, CO: Lynne Rienner Publishers, 2000.

Gagnon, V. P., Jr. "Ethnic Nationalism and International Conflict: The Case of Serbia." *International Security* 19, no. 3 (winter 1994–1995): 130–166.

Ginifer, Jeremy, ed. "Beyond the Emergency: Development Within UN Peace Missions." *International Peacekeeping* 3, no. 2, special issue (summer 1996).

Glenny, Misha. *The Fall of Yugoslavia: The Third Balkan War.* New York: Penguin, 1993.

———. "Decision Time in Bosnia." *New York Times,* 8 September 1996: 17.

Guest, Iain. "Moving Beyond Ethnic Conflict: Community Peace Building in Bosnia and Eastern Slavonia (Croatia)." Paper presented at the USAID conference "Promoting Democracy, Human Rights, and Reintegration in Post-conflict Societies." Washington, DC, 30–31 October 1997.

Harris, Peter, and Ben Reilly, eds. *Democracy and Deep-Rooted Conflict: Options for Negotiators.* Stockholm, Sweden: International Institute for Democracy and Electoral Assistance (IDEA), 1998.

Henkin, Alice H., ed. "Honoring Human Rights: From Peace to Justice: Recommendations to the International Community." Washington, DC: Aspen Institute, Justice and Society Program, 1998.

Hertić, Zlatko, Amela Sapčanin, and Susan Woodward. "Bosnia and Herzegovina." In Shepard Forman and Stewart Patrick, eds., *Good Intentions: Pledges of Aid for Postconflict Recovery.* Center on International Cooperation Studies in Multilateralism. Boulder, CO: Lynne Rienner Publishers, 2000.

Hoare, Attila. "A Rope Supports a Man Who Is Hanged—NATO Air Strikes and the End of Bosnian Resistance." *East European Politics and Societies* 12, no. 2 (spring 1998): 203–221.

Holbrooke, Richard C. *To End a War.* New York: Random House, 1998.

Hooper, Rick, and Mark Taylor. "Command from the Saddle: Managing United Nations Peace-building Missions. Recommendations Report of the Forum on the Special Representative of the Secretary-General: Shaping the UN's Role in Peace Implementation." Fafo Report 266. Oslo, Norway: Fafo Institute for Applied Social Science, 1999.

Human Rights Watch/Helsinki Reports. Available online at http://www. hrw.org/pubweb/Webcat–15.htm#P511_89987.

International Commission on the Balkans. *Unfinished Peace: Report of the International Commission on the Balkans.* Foreword by Leo Tindemans. Washington, DC: Carnegie Endowment for International Peace, 1996.

International Criminal Tribunal for the Former Yugoslavia. Documents and reporting available online at http://www.un.org/icty.

International Crisis Group. "Bosnia Reports." Available online at www. crisisweb.org.

Jones, Bruce D. *Peacemaking in Rwanda: The Dynamics of Failure.* Boulder, CO: Lynne Rienner Publishers, forthcoming.

Joulwan, George A., and Christopher C. Shoemaker. *Civilian-Military Cooperation in the Prevention of Deadly Conflict: Implementing Agreements in Bosnia and Beyond.* New York: Carnegie Commission on Preventing Deadly Conflict, December 1998.

Kaufman, Stuart. "The Irresistible Force and the Imperceptible Object: The Yugoslav Breakup and Western Policy." *Security Studies* 4, no. 2 (winter 1994–1995): 281–329.

Kostakos, Georgios. "Division of Labor Among International Organizations: The Bosnian Experience." *Global Governance* 4, no. 1 (October–December 1998): 461–484.

Kühne, Winrich. *Winning the Peace: Concept and Lessons Learned of Post-conflict Peacebuilding.* Ebenhausen, Germany: Research Institute for International Affairs, July 1996.

Kühne, Winrich, Cord Meier-Klodt, and Christina Meinecke. *The Transition from Peacekeeping to Peacebuilding: Planning, Coordination and Funding in the Twilight Zone, Berlin Follow-up Workshop: New York, 10 March 1997.* Ebenhausen, Germany: Stiftung Wissenschaft und Politik, 1997.

Kumar, Krishna, ed. *Rebuilding Societies After Civil War: Critical Roles for International Assistance.* Boulder, CO: Lynne Rienner Publishers, 1997.

———. *Post-conflict Elections, Democratization, and International Assistance.* Boulder, CO: Lynne Rienner Publishers, 1998.

Lake, David A., and Donald Rothchild. *Ethnic Fears and Global Engagement: The International Spread and Management of Ethnic Conflict.* Policy Paper 20. San Diego: University of California Institute on Global Conflict and Cooperation, January 1996.

Lepgold, Joseph. "NATO's Post–Cold War Collective Action Problem." *International Security* 23, no. 1 (summer 1998): 78–106.

Licklider, Roy. "The Consequences of Negotiated Settlements in Civil Wars, 1945–1993." *American Political Science Review* 89, no. 3 (September 1995): 681–687.

———. "Early Returns: Results of the First Wave of Statistical Studies of Civil War Termination." *Civil Wars* 1, no. 3 (autumn 1998): 120–132.

Malcolm, Noel. *Bosnia: A Short History.* London: Macmillan, 1994.

Nowak, Manfred. "Lessons for the International Human Rights Regime from the Yugoslav Experience." *Collected Courses of the Academy of European Law,* vol. 8, book 2. The Hague: Kluwer Law International, 2000.

Oakley, Robert B., Michael J. Dziedzic, and Eliot M. Goldberg, eds. *Policing the New World Disorder: Peace Operations and Public Security.* Washington, DC: National Defense University Press, 1998.

Office of the High Representative. Documents and reporting available online at http://www.ohr.int.

O'Flaherty, Michael, and Gregory Gisvold, eds. *Post War Protection of Human Rights in Bosnia and Herzegovina*. Boston: M. Nijhoff Publishers, 1998.

Owen, David. *Balkan Odyssey*. New York: Harcourt Brace, 1995.

Pajić, Zoran. "A Critical Appraisal of Human Rights Provisions of the Dayton Constitution of Bosnia and Herzegovina." *Human Rights Quarterly* 20 (1998): 125–138.

Paris, Roland. "Peacebuilding and the Limits of Liberal Internationalism." *International Security* 22, no. 2 (fall 1997): 54–89.

Peck, Connie. *Sustainable Peace: The Role of the UN and Regional Organizations in Preventing Conflict*. Washington, DC: Carnegie Commission on Preventing Deadly Conflict; and Lanham, MD: Rowman and Littlefield, 1998.

Posen, Barry R. "The Security Dilemma and Ethnic Conflict." In Michael E. Brown, ed., *Ethnic Conflict and International Security*. Princeton: Princeton University Press, 1993.

Radio Free Europe/Radio Liberty Newsline. Available online at http://www.rferl.org/newsline/.

Ratner, Steven R. *The New UN Peacekeeping: Building Peace in Lands of Conflict After the Cold War*. New York: St. Martin's Press, 1995.

Roberts, Adam. "Communal Conflict as a Challenge to International Organization: The Case of Former Yugoslavia." *Review of International Studies* 21 (1995): 389–410.

Rohde, David. *Endgame: The Betrayal and Fall of Srebrenica, Europe's Worst Massacre Since World War II*. New York: Farrar, Straus and Giroux, 1997.

Rose, Gideon. "Exit Strategy Delusion." *Foreign Affairs* (January–February 1998): 56–67.

Rothstein, Robert, ed. *After the Peace: Resistance and Reconciliation*. Boulder, CO: Lynne Rienner Publishers, 1999.

Rotberg, Robert I., ed. *Vigilance and Vengeance: NGOs Preventing Ethnic Conflict in Divided Societies*. Washington, DC: Brookings Institution Press; and Cambridge, MA: World Peace Foundation, 1996.

Rubin, Barney R., ed. *Toward Comprehensive Peace in Southeast Europe: Conflict Prevention in the South Balkans*. Report of the South Balkans Working Group of the Council on Foreign Relations Center for Preventive Action. New York: Twentieth Century Fund Press, 1996.

Schear, James. "Bosnia's Post-Dayton Traumas." *Foreign Policy* 104 (fall 1996): 87–101.

Sell, Louis. "The Serb Flight from Sarajevo: Dayton's First Failure." *Eastern European Politics and Societies* 14, no. 1 (winter 2000): 179–202.

Serwer, Daniel. "A Bosnian Federation Memoir." In Chester A. Crocker, Fen Osler Hampson, and Pamela Aall, eds., *Herding Cats: Multiparty Mediation in a Complex World*. Washington, DC: United States Institute of Peace Press, 1999.

Sharp, Jane M. O. "Dayton Report Card. *International Security* 22, no. 3 (winter 1997–1998): 101–137.

Silber, Laura, and Allan Little. *Yugoslavia: Death of a Nation*. New York: TV Books, 1995.

Singer, Peter W. "Bosnia 2000: Phoenix or Flames?" *World Policy Journal* 17, no. 1 (spring 2000): 31–38.

Sisk, Tim. *Powersharing and International Mediation in Ethnic Conflicts.* Washington, DC: U.S. Institute for Peace, 1996.

Stedman, Stephen John. "Spoiler Problems in Peace Processes." *International Security* 22, no. 2 (fall 1997): 5–53.

Stedman, Stephen John, Donald Rothchild, and Elizabeth M. Cousens, eds. *Strategies, Organizations and Consequences: Explaining the Outcome of Peace Implementation in Civil Wars.* Vol. 2 of "Ending Civil Wars," a joint research project of the Center for International Security and Co-operation and the International Peace Academy. Unpublished manuscript.

Steil, Benn, and Susan L. Woodward. "A European New Deal for the Balkans." *Foreign Affairs* (November–December 1999): 95–105.

Szasz, Paul C. "Protecting Human and Minority Rights in Bosnia: A Documentary Survey of International Proposals." *California Western International Law Journal* 25, no. 2 (spring 1995): 237–310.

———. "The Protection of Human Rights Through the Dayton/Paris Peace Agreement on Bosnia." *American Journal of International Law* 90, no. 2 (April 1996): 301–316.

Thompson, Mark. *A Paper House: The Ending of Yugoslavia.* New York: Pantheon Books, 1992.

Thornberry, Cedric. "Saving the War Crimes Tribunal." *Foreign Policy* 104 (fall 1996): 72–86.

Ullman, Richard H., ed. *The World and Yugoslavia's Wars.* New York: Council on Foreign Relations, 1996.

U.S. Committee for Refugees. *World Refugee Survey.* Annual country reports for Bosnia and Herzegovina, available online at http://www.refugees.org/world/countryindex/bosnia_herce.htm.

Weiss Fagen, Patricia. "After the Conflict: A Review of Selected Sources on Rebuilding War-torn Societies." Occasional Paper no. 1, War-torn Societies Project. Geneva: UNRISD, November 1995.

Williams, Michael C. *Civil-Military Relations and Peacekeeping.* Adelphi Paper no. 321. London: International Institute for Strategic Studies, 1998.

Woods, Ngaire. "Good Governance in International Organizations." *Global Governance* (January–March 1999): 39–62.

Woodward, David. *The IMF, the World Bank, and Economic Policy in Bosnia.* Oxford: Oxfam, 1998.

Woodward, Susan L. *Balkan Tragedy: Chaos and Dissolution After the Cold War.* Washington, DC: Brookings Institution, 1995.

———. "Implementing Peace in Bosnia and Herzegovina: A Post-Dayton Primer and Memorandum of Warning." Brookings Discussion Papers. Washington, DC: Brookings Institution, May 1996.

———. "America's Bosnia Policy: The Work Ahead." Brookings Institution Policy Brief no. 2. Washington, DC: Brookings Institution, July 1996.

———. "Compromised Sovereignty to Create Sovereignty: Is Dayton a Futile Exercise or an Emerging Model?" Washington, DC: Brookings Institution, unpublished paper.

Zimmerman, Warren. *Origins of a Catastrophe: Yugoslavia and Its Destroyers—America's Last Ambassador Tells What Happened and Why.* New York: Times Books, 1996.

REFERENCE AND NEWS

The following sources, official and unofficial, can be relied upon for accurate reporting and insightful analysis about developments in Bosnia.

Economist Intelligence Unit. Country Profiles and Country Reports for Bosnia-Herzegovina. London: Economic Intelligence Unit, Ltd.

European Stability Initiative Publications. Available online at http://www.esiweb.org/hauptseite.html.

Human Rights Watch/Helsinki Reports. Available online at http://www.hrw.org/pubweb/Webcat-15.htm#P511_89987.

International Criminal Tribunal for the Former Yugoslavia. Documents and reporting. Available online at http://www.un.org/icty.

International Crisis Group. Bosnia Reports. Available online at www.crisisweb.org.

International Institute of Strategic Studies. Annual, The Military Balance. London: Oxford University Press.

Office of the High Representative. Documents and reporting. Available online at http://www.ohr.int.

Radio Free Europe/Radio Liberty Newsline. Available online at http://www.rferl. org/newsline/.

Stockholm International Peace Research Institute. Annual, Yearbook: Armaments, Disarmament and International Security. New York: Oxford University Press.

United States Committee for Refugees. Country Reports: Bosnia and Herzegovina. Annual, World Refugee Survey. Availabe online at http://www.refugees.org/ world/countryindex/ bosnia_herce.htm.

AUTHOR INTERVIEWS, 1996–1999

Where individuals have been interviewed multiple times, we have tried to include all dates. Where contact has been made frequently, we refer to key dates only. Position and affiliation of the person interviewed are given as at the time of the main interview. All interviews conducted by Elizabeth M. Cousens.

Al Alfi, Hussein. Deputy Head of Civil Affairs, UNMIBH, Sarajevo (11–19 November 1996).

Al-Hussein, Zeid Ra'ad. Deputy Permanent Representative, Permanent Mission to the United Nations of the Hashemite Kingdom of Jordan, New York (5 March 1997).

Almstrom, John. Head of Civil Affairs, UNMIBH, Sarajevo (11–19 November 1996).

Amneus, Henrik. Principal Adviser on Human Rights, UNTAES, Vukovar (24–27 November 1996).

Anic, Mijo. Mayor of Ravne Brcko, Ravne Brcko (23 November 1996).

Arretti, Michael. International Organizations, U.S. Department of State, Washington, D.C. (October 1996).

Ashton, Barry W. Former Deputy Commander, UNPROFOR, Ithaca, New York (26 April 1997).

Avdic, Sead. Vice-Mayor of Tuzla, Tuzla (21–22 November 1996).

Balian, Hrair. Director, International Crisis Group, Sarajevo (7 March 1998).

Barber, Martin. Deputy Special Representative of the Secretary-General, UNMIBH, Sarajevo (11–19 November 1996).

Barry, Robert. Head of Mission, OSCE, Sarajevo (11 August 1998).

Baskin, Mark. Political Advisor, UNTAES, Vukovar (24–27 November 1996); Political Advisor, UNMIBH, Sarajevo (6 March 1998; 7 August 1998).

Beaumont, Geoff. Civil Affairs Officer, UNMIBH Liaison Office, Pale (18 November 1996).

Bender, Ivan. President, District Assembly of Neretva Canton; Chairman, House of Representatives of Croatian Republic of Herzeg-Bosna, Mostar (13–14 November 1996).

Bennett, Christopher. International Crisis Group, Sarajevo (11–19 November 1996; 4–5 March 1998).

Bet-El, Ilana. Civil Affairs Officer, UNMIBH, Sarajevo (11–19 November 1996).

Bettyar, Ivan. Regional Civil Affairs Coordinator, UNMIBH, Banja Luka (19–20 November 1996).

Binda, Francesca. Director, National Democratic Institute, Sarajevo (12 August 1998).

Bolling, Landrum. Director at Large, Mercy Corps/Scottish European Aid, Sarajevo (11–19 November 1996).

Boothby, Derek. Deputy Transitional Administrator, UNTAES, Vukovar (24–27 November 1996).

Calver, Richard. Political Affairs Officer, UN Liaison Office, Zagreb (6–11 November 1996).

Campbell, Leslie. Director, National Democratic Institute, Toronto (March 1997).

Cardones-Ramon, Ramon. Civil Affairs Officer, UNMIBH, Mostar (13–14 November 1996).

Carter, J. Deputy Officer-in-Charge, UN Liaison Office, Zagreb (6–11 November 1996).

Chayes, Antonia Handler. Head, Conflict Management Group, Cambridge, Mass. (October 1996).

Cicak, Ivan Zvomimir. Director, Helsinki Committee, Zagreb (6–11 November 1996).

Clages, Christian. Deputy High Representative for Political Affairs, OHR, Sarajevo (3–4 August 1998).

Colliver, Sandra. Legal Adviser, International Crisis Group, Sarajevo (March 1998).

Cordone, Claudio. Head of Human Rights Unit, UNMIBH, Sarajevo (5 March 1998).

Cubbon, John. Legal Officer, UNMIBH, Sarajevo (7 March 1998).

Day, Graham M. Chief, Civil Affairs Training Unit, UNMIBH, Sarajevo (31 July 1998).

de Vargas, François. Human Rights Officer, OSCE, Brcko (23 November 1996).

Demichelis, Julia. Washington, D.C. (31 October 1997).

Denitch, Bogdan. New York University (March 1996 and following).

Derajic, Svjetlana. Project Manager, International Council of Voluntary Agencies, Sarajevo (11–19 November 1996).

Djurdjevic, Vlado. Chief of Police, Doboj (22 November 1996).

Dolar, Antonia. Head of Civil Affairs, Tuzla, UNMIBH, Tuzla (21–22 November 1996).

Dreyer, Ronald. Head of the Electoral Office, OSCE, Brcko (23 November 1996).

Dufour, Patrice. The World Bank, Sarajevo (4 August 1998).

Dukic, Zlatko. Cantonal President (SDP), Tuzla (21–22 November 1996).

Dvornik, Srdan. Managing Director, Open Society Institute, Zagreb (6–11 November 1996).

Eide, Vigglik. Ambassador of Norway to the Syrian Arab Republic, New York (October 1996).

Fall, Merrick. Civil Affairs Officer, UNMIBH, Brcko (November 23, 1996).

Fischer, Gerard A. Head of Civil Affairs, UNTAES, Vukovar (24–27 November 1996).

FitzGerald, Peter. Commissioner, IPTF, Sarajevo (11–19 November 1996).

Fitzpatrick, Michael. United States Department of State, Washington, D.C. (October 1996).

Gajic, Goran. Secretary, Local Electoral Commission, Brcko (23 November 1996).

Galbraith, Peter W. U.S. Ambassador to Croatia, Ithaca, New York (26 April 1997).

Garrod, Sir Martin. EU Special Envoy, Mostar (13–14 November 1996).

Gonzaga, A. Field Officer, UNHCR, Brcko (23 November 1996).

Grinberg, Jaques. Head of Political Unit, UNTAES, Vukovar (24–27 November 1996).

Grubisa, Damir. Director, Croatia Peace Research Institute, Zagreb (6–11 November 1996).

Guest, Iain. United States Institute of Peace, Washington D.C. (30 October 1997 and following).

Hamilton, Angelika. Office of the High Representative, Sarajevo (11–19 November 1996).

Hampton, Randall. Elections Officer, OSCE, Brcko (23 November 1996).

Harland, David. Head of Civil Affairs, UNMIBH, Sarajevo (March 1998 and following).

Harvey, Joanna. Human Rights and NGO Relations Officer, OHR Region West, Banja Luka (19–20 November 1996).

Haukland, H. Senior Military Liaison Officer, UNMIBH, Sarajevo (11–19 November 1996).

Herdina, Andreas. Office of the High Representative, Sarajevo (11–19 November 1996).

Hicks, Peggy. Human Rights Officer, OHR, Sarajevo (11–19 November 1996); Deputy High Representative for Human Rights, OHR, Sarajevo (9–10 August 1998).

Hunt, Angelika. Civil Affairs Officer, UNMIBH, Banja Luka (19–20 November 1996).

Hwon, James. Civil Affairs Officer, UNTAES, Vukovar (24–27 November 1996).

IFOR Briefing, Colonel Reddish and Major Ciminelli, Camp McGovern, Brcko (November 23, 1996); Lt. Aaberg, Nordpol Brigade HQ, Tuzla (November 1996).

Ivanic, Mladen. Former Member of Bosnian Presidency, Pale (18 November 1996).

Ivanko, Alexander. Spokesman, UNMIBH, Sarajevo (5 March 1998).

Jahic, Hamdija. President, City Council, Mostar (13–14 November 1996).

Jarvenpää, Minna. Refugee and Humanitarian Affairs Officer, OHR, Sarajevo (11–19 November 1996).

Jerkic, Zejlko. Counsellor, Permanent Mission of the Republic of Bosnia and Herzegovina to the United Nations, New York (October 1996).

Johnson, Mark. Civil Affairs Officer, UNMIBH, Doboj (22 November 1996).

Jones, Lisa. UNHCR, Sarajevo (12 August 1998).

Jones, Peter. Chief of Staff, Office of the SRSG, UNMIBH, Sarajevo (11–19 November 1996; 3 March 1998).

Jovanovic, Vladislav. Permanent Representative, Permanent Mission of the Federal Republic of Yugoslavia to the United Nations, New York (October 1996).

Katic, Ivo. Chief of Police, Usora (23 November 1996).

Kauzerlich, Richard. Ambassador of the United States to Bosnia and Herzegovina, Sarajevo (9 August 1998).

Klein, Jacques Paul. Transitional Administrator, UNTAES, Vukovar (24–27 November 1996); Principal Deputy High Representative, OHR, Sarajevo (5 March 1998).

Kojic, President, Serb Democratic Party; President, Brcko Municipal Assembly, Brcko (23 November 1996).

Komarica, Franjo. Roman Catholic Bishop of Banja Luka, Banja Luka (19–20 November 1996).

Korula, Anna R. Human Rights Officer, Deputy Chair, Joint Implementation Committee on Human Rights, UNTAES, Vukovar (24–27 November 1996).

Kramaric, Zlatko. Mayor of Osijek; Vice President, Croatian Social Liberal Party, Osijek (25 November 1996).

Krnjajic, Sanja. Director, Youth Center, Gornji Vakuf (9 March 1998).

Kroeker, Mark. Deputy Commissioner, IPTF, Sarajevo (5 March 1998).

Lebedev, Alexander. Head of Mission, UN Liaison Office, Zagreb (6–11 November 1996).

Leho, Fatima. Governor, Neretva Canton, Mostar (13–14 November 1996).

Levi, Zoran. Helsinki Citizens Assembly, Banja Luka (19–20 November 1996).

Maclay, Michael. Chief Spokesman and Special Advisor, OHR, Sarajevo (11–19 November 1996).

Malloch Brown, Mark. Vice President, External Affairs, World Bank (October 1996).

Mandhyam, Kishore. Civil Affairs Officer, UNTAES, Vukovar (24–27 November 1996).

Martinico, Joe. Director, International Council of Voluntary Agencies, Banja Luka (November 1996); Regional Coordinator, UNDP Village Environmental Employment Project, Sarajevo (August 3, 1998).

McKinley, Brunson. Bosnia Humanitarian Coordinator, United States Department of State, Washington, D.C. (October 1996).

Miljevic, Damir. Head, Social-Liberal Party, Banja Luka (19–20 November 1996).

Miller, Laura. Fellow, Olin Institute, Cambridge, Mass. (October 1996).

Monk, Richard. Commissioner, IPTF, Sarajevo (9 August 1998).

Morris, Eric. Deputy SRSG, UNMIBH, Sarajevo (13 August 1998).

Nobilo, Mario. Permanent Representative, Permanent Mission of the Republic of Croatia to the United Nations, New York (October 1996).

Orucevic, Safet. Deputy Mayor, Mostar (13–14 November 1996).

Peterson, Jeannie. Head of Civil Affairs, Vinkovci (24–27 November 1996).

Phillips, David. Executive Director, International Conflict Resolution Program, Columbia University, New York (June 1997 and following).

Pierce, Philip. UN Development Programme, Sarajevo (11–19 November 1996); Travnik (9 March 1998).

Pitter, Laura. Policy Officer, IPTF, Sarajevo (5 March 1998).

Platzer, Michael K. H. Head, UN Office in Vienna, New York (March 1996); Sarajevo (11–19 November 1996).

Poplasen, Nikola. President, Serb Radical Party; Deputy Speaker, RS Parliament, Banja Luka (19–20 November 1996).

Price, John. Desk Officer for Serbia and Montenegro, United States Department of State, Washington, D.C. (October 1996).

Puljic, Mile. President, Croatian Democratic Union, Mostar (13–14 November 1996).

Radic, Predrag. Former Mayor of Banja Luka; Head, Union for Peace and Progress, Banja Luka (19–20 November 1996).

Radisic, Zivko. Banja Luka (19–20 November 1996).

Rehn, Elisabeth. SRSG, UNMIBH, Sarajevo (6 March 1998).

Rieff, David. Writer, New York (October 1996 and following).

Sacirbey, Muhamed. Permanent Representative, Permanent Mission to the United Nations of the Republic of Bosnia and Herzegovina, New York (3 November 1997 and following).

Sajnovic, Snjezane. Administrator, Center for Peace, Non-violence and Human Rights, Osijek (25 November 1996).

Sargent, Keith. Ministry of Foreign Affairs of Bosnia-Herzegovina, Sarajevo (11–19 November 1996).

Scarlett, Earle St. Auban. Former Senior Political Adviser to the High Representative, Washington, D.C. (October 1996).

Schear, James. Senior Associate, Carnegie Endowment for International Peace, Washington, D.C. (October 1996).

Schein, Deborah. Electoral Adviser, OHR, Sarajevo (10 August 1998).

Schmitt, Thomas. Political Adviser, OHR, Sarajevo (11–19 November 1996).

Shitakha, Emma. Officer for Bosnia and Herzegovina, UN Department of Peace-keeping Operations, New York (October 1996).

Silovic, Darko. Former Permanent Representative of the Federal Republic of Yugoslavia to the United Nations, New York (October 1996 and following).

Silovic, Dasa. New York (October 1996 and following).

Stoltenberg, Thorvald. New York (October 1996).

Sukic, Krunoslav. Secretary, Center for Peace, Non-violence and Human Rights, Osijek (November 25, 1996).

Szasz, Paul C. Former Senior Legal Adviser to ICFY, Ithaca, New York (25–27 April 1997 and following).

Tepper, Lisa. Desk Officer for Croatia, United States Department of State, Washington, D.C. (October 1996).

Thompson, Mark. Head of Media Analysis Unit, UN Liaison Office, Zagreb (6–11 November 1996).

Toivonen, Jarkko. District Commander, IPTF, Doboj (22 November 1996).

Tull, Stephen. Political Adviser, UNTAES , Beli Manastir (November 1996).

Vasak, Kristina. Human Rights Officer, OHR Region West, Banja Luka (19–20 November 1996).

Vuco, Beka. Open Society Institute, New York (October 1996).

Waheedullah, Waheed. Head of Civil Affairs, Mostar, UNMIBH, Mostar (13–14 November 1996).

Walker, Catherine. Deputy Chief of Mission, UNHCR, Sarajevo (11–19 November 1996).

Walker, Stephen W. Associate Director, Balkan Institute, Ithaca, New York (25–27 April 1997).

Wasserman, Robert. Deputy Commissioner, IPTF, Sarajevo (11–19 November 1996).

Williams, Peter. Chief Faction Liaison Officer, SFOR, Sarajevo (9 August 1998).

Woodward, Susan. Senior Fellow, The Brookings Institution, Washington, D.C. (October 1996); Senior Adviser, OSCE Mission to Bosnia and Herzegovina, Sarajevo (August 1998 and following).

Zeciragic, Fedad. Legal Expert, Office of the Ombudsman, Human Rights Commission for Bosnia and Herzegovina, Sarajevo (9 August 1998).

Zivanovic, Lidia. Director, Helsinki Citizens' Assembly, Banja Luka (19–20 November 1996).

Index

Agreement on Sub-Regional Arms
Control (June 1996). *See* Florence
Agreement
Agriculture, 91
Aid: conditionality, 81–82, 96, 104,
144; for economic recovery, 88–89,
95; military, 54, 56; to Republika
Srpska, 98*n26*
Albright, Madeleine, 67*n25,* 130
Angola, 139, 148*n7*
Arizona market, 149*n10*
Arms control, 38, 49*n3,* 54–55
Arms embargos, 29*n22*
Army of Bosnia and Herzegovina
(ABiH), 55, 57, 64
Army of Republika Srpska (VRS), 56,
64
Arusha Accords, 148*n7*
Austria, 108*n12*
Authoritarianism, 26

Baker, James, 28*n15*
Banja Luka, 26
Barry, Robert, 123
Bildt, Carl, 51*n22,* 113
Blair, Tony, 67*n25,* 130
Bonn powers, 125*n12,* 130–131, 147
Boothby, Derek, 138
Bosic, Boro, 108*n6*
Bosnia: ethnicity in, 19, 21; govern-
ment, 102–103; independence, 19;
integration of Bosnian communities,
15, 44, 131, 143; judicial system of,
120, 127*n38,* 142; partition of,
34–35
Bosnia, economy of: aid for recovery,

88–89, 95; corruption, 95; Dayton
Agreement effect on, 87–88; foreign
debt, 88, 92–93; interentity trade,
149*n10;* monetary and fiscal policy,
94; physical reconstruction, 89–90;
political constraints on, 96–97; positive developments, 141; postwar
development, 90–92; prewar decline
in, 87; privatization, 94–95, 97,
99*n42;* transition to capitalism, 141;
war's effect on, 25, 31*n35,* 87
Bosnia, international actors in: allocation of roles for, 146; military
responsibilities, 37; rivalry among,
45; U.S. political constraints on, 46
Bosnia, military forces in: separation of,
54, 65, 143; troop strength, 16*n2,* 55,
66*n4;* withdrawal of foreign combatants, 53–54
Bosnia, peacebuilding in: Dayton
Agreement role of, 36–37, 45–46;
hierarchy of goals in, 138– 139; sovereignty vs. international authority,
147–148, 151–153; trusteeship
model for, 129–134; U.S. military
involvement, 46, 49
Bosnia, security in: arms control,
54–55; consolidating the cease-fire,
53–54; extramilitary forces, 36,
57–59; police role in, 59–61; protection of civilians, 53, 62–64; separation of forces, 54; train and equip
program, 55–57, 67*n14*
Bosniac-Croat Federation: currency
used in, 94; Dayton Agreement provisions for, 36, 45, 102; economy of,

179

About this Publication

When the Dayton peace agreement was signed in 1995, there were expectations among the signatories, the Bosnian population, and the international community alike that the pact would not only end conflict among Bosnia's three armies but also establish a political and social foundation for more robust peace. Recognizing that the latter goal—incorporating political reform and democratization, consolidating a multiethnic state, and providing for economic reconstruction and development—remains significantly unmet, Cousens and Cater explore the reasons for the only limited success.

Was the agreement fundamentally flawed, or has the disappointing progress been more attributable to weaknesses in implementation? The authors examine the choices made, as well as the constraints faced, by those seeking a lasting peace in Bosnia.

Elizabeth M. Cousens is director of research at the International Peace Academy. Her current work focuses on comparative peace implementation in the context of civil war. **Charles K. Cater** is a doctoral student in international relations at the University of Oxford. Previously, he was a program officer in the research program of the International Peace Academy.

Other International Peace Academy Publications

Available from Lynne Rienner Publishers, 1800 30th Street, Boulder, Colorado 80301 (303-444-6684), www.rienner.com:

Rights and Reconciliation: UN Strategies in El Salvador, Ian Johnstone (1995)

Building Peace in Haiti, Chetan Kumar (1998)

Greed and Grievance: Economic Agendas in Civil War, edited by Mats Berdal and David Malone (2000)

The Sanctions Decade: Assessing UN Strategies in the 1990s, David Cortright and George A. Lopez (2000)

Peacebuilding as Politics: Cultivating Peace in Fragile Societies, edited by Elizabeth M. Cousens and Chetan Kumar (2001)

Sierra Leone: Diamonds and the Struggle for Democracy, John L. Hirsch (2001)

Civilians in War, edited by Simon Chesterman (2001)

Peacemaking in Rwanda: The Dynamics of Failure, Bruce D. Jones (2001)

Kosovo: An Unfinished Peace, William G. O'Neill (2001)

From Reaction to Conflict Prevention: Opportunities for the UN System, edited by Fen Osler Hampson and David M. Malone (2002)

The International Peace Academy

The International Peace Academy (IPA) is an independent, nonpartisan, international institution devoted to the promotion of peaceful and multilateral approaches to the resolution of international as well as internal conflicts. IPA plays a facilitating role in efforts to settle conflicts, providing a middle ground where the options for settling particular conflicts are explored and promoted in an informal setting. Other activities of the organization include public forums; training seminars on conflict resolution and peacekeeping; and research and workshops on collective security, regional and internal conflicts, peacemaking, peacekeeping, and nonmilitary aspects of security.

In fulfilling its mission, IPA works closely with the United Nations, regional and other organizations, governments, and parties to conflicts. The work of IPA is further enhanced by its ability to draw on a worldwide network of eminent persons including government leaders, statesmen, business leaders, diplomats, military officers, and scholars. In the decade following the end of the Cold War, there has been a general awakening to the enormous potential of peaceful and multilateral approaches to resolving conflicts. This has given renewed impetus to the role of IPA.

IPA is governed by an international board of directors. Financial support for the work of the organization is provided primarily by philanthropic foundations, as well as individual donors.